The opinions and experiences of autistic c
all too often overlooked in autism rese;
inspiring book puts that right, by placir
centre of discussion. Goodall's deep respect for, and willingness to listen
to and learn from the young autistic people in his research is exemplary.
Everyone with an interest in autism should read it.

Professor Liz Pellicano, Macquarie University, Sydney, Australia

Recently, there has been an increased emphasis on developing appropriate educational responses for children and young people on the
autism spectrum. However, there are relatively few books that provide
in-depth insights into the lives of young people on the autism spectrum
as they navigate their school journeys. Craig Goodall's book addresses
this serious gap in the literature through a scholarly yet grounded piece
of work. Craig has adopted a creative research approach designed to
support and empower these young people. Their stories, their struggles
and their successes are at the heart of this book. This is essential reading
for practitioners, policymakers and all those interested in developing
inclusive learning environments as we begin to learn about how the
voices of these young people can be recognised and help us to recon-
ceptualise school life so that these young people can be fully included.

**Michael Shevlin, Professor in Inclusive Education, School of Education
and Director of Trinity Centre for People with Intellectual Disabilities,
Trinity College Dublin, Ireland**

This is a highly important and insightful book on the educational
experiences of a group of young people who have, for too long, been
rendered invisible by dominant educational pedagogy. In this key text for
educators, trainee teachers, researchers and policymakers, Goodall
exposes us to the rich possibilities and practicalities of participatory and
rights-based research in accessing autistic young people's perspectives.
The findings force us as researchers and educators to engage critically
with inclusive education discourse and its emergent tensions, not least
the implications for policy and practice. These voices cannot and should
not be ignored.

**Dr Bronagh Byrne, Lecturer in Social Policy, Programme Director for
MSc Children's Rights, School of Social Sciences, Education and Social
Work, Queen's University, Belfast, Northern Ireland**

Understanding the Voices and Educational Experiences of Autistic Young People

Providing a 'one stop' text, *Understanding the Voices and Educational Experiences of Autistic Young People* is a unique and comprehensive contribution to bridge the gap between theory, research and practice. Based on the author's teaching and research experience, this book provides a theoretical and practical framework for participatory rights-based autism research and demonstrates the benefits of – and growing emphasis on – voice and participation research; if done correctly it can be of immense benefit to policy, practice and how we support autistic young people.

Alongside a critical and extensive review of research literature and debate on the efficacy of mainstream inclusion for autistic children, the book provides practical advice on how to support autistic children in research and in school. Significantly, Goodall investigates and presents the educational experiences of autistic young people – including girls – and their suggestions to improve educational practice from their own perspectives, as opposed to adult stakeholders.

This book will act as a key text for student teachers, practitioner-researchers, those already supporting autistic children in education or social settings (including teachers, school leaders, special education leads, policymakers) and academics researching in the areas of autism and inclusion.

Dr Craig Goodall is an educator with 12 years' experience working with autistic young people and others out of mainstream education in Northern Ireland, UK.

Routledge Research in Special Educational Needs

This series provides a forum for established and emerging scholars to discuss the latest debates, research and practice in the evolving field of Special Educational Needs.

Books in the series include:

Understanding the Voices and Educational Experiences of Autistic Young People
From Research to Practice
By Craig Goodall

The Global Convergence of Vocational and Special Education
Mass Schooling and Modern Educability
By John G. Richardson, Jinting Wu, and Douglas M. Judge

Adult Interactive Style Intervention and Participatory Research Designs in Autism
Bridging the Gap between Academic Research and Practice
By Lila Kossyvaki

For more information about this series, please visit: www.routledge.com/ Routledge-Research-in-Special-Educational-Needs/book-series/RRSEN

Understanding the Voices and Educational Experiences of Autistic Young People
From Research to Practice

Craig Goodall

Routledge
Taylor & Francis Group
LONDON AND NEW YORK

First published 2020
by Routledge
2 Park Square, Milton Park, Abingdon, Oxon OX14 4RN

and by Routledge
52 Vanderbilt Avenue, New York, NY 10017

Routledge is an imprint of the Taylor & Francis Group, an informa business

First issued in paperback 2021

British Library Cataloguing-in-Publication Data
A catalogue record for this book is available from the British Library

Library of Congress Cataloging-in-Publication Data
A catalog record has been requested for this book

ISBN: 978-0-367-25325-7 (hbk)
ISBN: 978-1-03-208961-4 (pbk)
ISBN: 978-0-429-28718-3 (ebk)

Typeset in Times New Roman
by Taylor & Francis Books

Contents

Figures

Tables

Acknowledgements

Thank you to Prof Laura Lundy and Dr Alison MacKenzie of Queen's University Belfast for their supervision throughout my Doctorate. Further thanks go to Dr MacKenzie for her expertise and advice when reviewing this book. Thank you to the 12 autistic young people who kindly shared their educational experiences. Finally, thank you to my wife and children for their support.

Preface

I have taught in an Alternative Education Provision (AEP) in Northern Ireland since 2007. From discussions with autistic young people I became aware that their mainstream educational experiences had, in the main, been negative, resulting in a refusal to attend school – anxiety based for many – and, for some, their behaviour was deemed too challenging for mainstream to support, resulting in exclusion. Bullying, anxiety, fear of the unknown, teachers who lacked understanding and a lack of flexibility have all been informally discussed by these young people. Outside school I began working with parents and learned that many of their autistic children have had similar experiences, resulting in some having to be withdrawn from formal education. This added to the picture that mainstream school may not be the most appropriate environment in which to meet the needs of all academically able autistic young people. Research conducted for my autism Master's degree indicated that teachers want and need more autism-specific training, but that the attitudes held are not always conducive to wanting to understand and engender inclusion.

In addition, my interest in children's rights, rights-based approaches and participatory autism research grew throughout my modules on the Doctorate of Education programme. I also explored the effectiveness of mainstream inclusion for autistic children and theories for developing inclusive practice. It became apparent that few studies have directly explored the educational experiences of autistic young people and their experiences of, and thoughts on, inclusion. Such a dearth of research means that there is very little rights-based qualitative participatory research exploring the perspectives of autistic young people themselves. Studies that do investigate these experiences generally do so through the lens of teachers or parents – the adults.

As a result, my resolve to afford autistic young people their right to be heard and participate in matters that impact on their lives (including research) from an approach that is not only rights respecting but rights enabling was strengthened. I judged that it was time to garner the educational experiences of these children and hopefully to use these insider narratives to inform policy and practice.

The school environment can be a hostile place for those who process the world differently. Thus, the educational experiences of these young people ought to be sought and used to inform school policy and practice, and gain deeper insight into mainstream inclusion for autistic learners.

In this book I not only present the experiences of these autistic young people but will guide readers through my Doctoral research, providing simple strategies and exploring decisions I made. Some of the issues I considered and overcame were guided by my experience working with many autistic young people and are not readily evident within research or educational texts. These methodological considerations will be assessed within a comprehensive discussion of extant literature relating to inclusion, rights, education and autism. A unique contribution to the field, this book – which will be of interest to educators (including trainee teachers and practitioner-researchers), undergraduate and postgraduate researchers, academics in education and psychology, educational policymakers, parents and autistic people themselves – will bridge the gaps between theory, research and practice. The book, structured across nine chapters, makes a valuable and comprehensive contribution to the field.

1 Setting the scene

Introduction

Autistic Spectrum Disorder (ASD) is described as the most prevalent of all neurodevelopmental disorders (Jang et al., 2014). ASD is formally characterised by a shared dyad of interacting challenges in social communication and repetitive behaviours, including difficulties (or differences) interacting with others and making sense of the social and sensory world. Although shared, this dyad is experienced differently by each individual and the term autism, a single word, attempts to encapsulate the experiences, characteristics and lives of many. By involving autistic young people in research, we will better understand their experiences of education and hopefully effect change in policy and practice.

This book bridges the gap between theory (the inclusion debate), research (understanding and supporting the voices of autistic young people) and practice (educational experience, school improvement and inclusion from the perspectives of autistic young people). I use this opening chapter to set the scene for what lies ahead. I explore historical perspectives on autism, how perceptions of autism are changing and the impact of the terminology we use for supporting autistic young people in education and research. As I will argue in this book, a lack of understanding, acceptance, support and unfriendly (school) environments exacerbate these challenges.

Historical perspectives

During the Second World War Leo Kanner (1943) studied 11 children of normal physical development and was the first to identify a definition for autism. According to him, the main features of this condition include severe social impairment, delayed speech development, impairments in communication, rigid thought processes and ritualistic patterns of behaviour. Kanner diagnosed these children as having 'Infantile Autism', or 'Kanner Syndrome'. In his classic paper *'Autistic Disturbance of Affect Contact'*, Kanner (1943, p.250) describes the children he studied as having 'come into the world with innate inability to form the usual, biologically provided affective contact with people'. This description would now be considered offensive, inaccurate and demeaning for many autistic people and their allies.

Hans Asperger (1944), also during the Second World War, worked with a similar group of children and identified a cluster that had social difficulties. However, in comparison to Kanner's group these children had average cognitive ability and displayed good verbal skills. These children are described as having 'Asperger Syndrome' (AS), a phrase first used by Wing (1981) and a condition Asperger himself is now considered to have had (Le Blanc and Volkers, 2008). Wing (1996) suggests that those with AS are sometimes known as having 'High Functioning Autism' – a divisive descriptor, as discussed below.

The work of Wing and Gould (1979) developed the concept that Kanner Syndrome, or autism, and AS could be part of a wider spectrum of disorders known as Autistic Spectrum Disorders. However, the concept of a spectrum is perhaps too linear and an over-simplistic representation of the diverse, changing nature and experiences of autistic people. The challenges faced can change from one situation to the next based on a multitude of social, sensory and environmental factors. The 'spectrum' can create the assumption of an undeviating scale ranging from a 'little autistic' to 'very autistic', thus pigeonholing autistic people into discrete, unchanging groups based on apparent, assumed static, levels of functioning; the low end and the high end of the spectrum – this is wonderfully illustrated by Rebecca Burgess (2016, www.rebecca burgess.co.uk). Caroline Hearst proposed a constellation model to represent the spiky, non-linear profiles and experiences of autistic people, which I also find useful (see www.autangel.org.uk/autism-constellation. html). I like to use a kaleidoscope analogy to represent the vast diversity and non-constant changing nature of autism for the individual. The importance of terminology and perception is revisited later.

Prevalence

Prevalence rates vary across countries and depend on diagnostic services, awareness amongst professionals and, ultimately, resources. The Department of Health, Social Services and Public Safety (2019) in Northern Ireland indicates that, in 2018/19, 3.3% of the school-aged population are autistic, an increase from 1.2% in 2008/09. This increase could be attributed to greater awareness amongst a range of professionals working with young people, such as teachers, an increase in diagnostic services and earlier identification. Wing (1997) suggests other possible reasons, such as an actual increase in the number of cases and a rise in other co-occurring disorders (with autism still being seen as a spectrum condition). Martin (2012) adds an increase in openness to seek a diagnosis in light of decreased social stigma attached to this list of reasons. To summarise, prevalence estimates have increased over time; this most likely represents changes in the concepts, definitions, service availability and awareness of autistic-spectrum disorders in both the lay and professional public.

Gender ratio and bias

Kreiser and White (2014) report a (relatively) consistent male bias of 4:1, although ratios vary across the spectrum, ranging from 2:1 in those with intellectual disabilities to 5.1:1 in those without (Kim et al., 2011). The DHSSPSNI (2019) indicates a ratio of 3.4:1, or 1.5% of females compared to 5.1% of males within the school-age population of Northern Ireland, although, according to Cooper, Smith and Russel (2018), a large proportion of autistic people do not align to the male/female binary position on gender, which makes determining gender ratios more difficult.

Autism is potentially under-identified in females without co-occurring learning difficulties. This may be due to subtle gender differences in the characteristics of autistic females compared to males, such as less unusual stereotyped and repetitive behaviours – or such behaviours being masked or camouflaged – coupled with a lack of autistic female research (Goodall and MacKenzie, 2018). Fletcher-Watson and Happé (2019, pp.42–43) also outline diagnostic overshadowing for females. They suggest:

> if clinicians don't think 'autism' when they meet a girl with social difficulties, they may think social anxiety, eating disorder or depression: diagnostic overshadowing occurs when clinicians stop at one presenting problem and don't go on to consider, for example, eating disorder *and* autism.

Professionals rely on observations and subjective judgements when deciding to make a diagnosis. Together these factors, arguably, give rise to gender bias in the diagnostic criteria used, which is difficult to uncover. Lai et al. (2015) propose that, in comparison to autistic males, females have better expressive behaviours, such as holding reciprocal conversations, and better initiation of interactions, but poorer main-tenance of these. Irrespective of the estimated ratios reported, literature suggests that ASD is predominantly diagnosed in males, with females being less likely to receive a diagnosis than males displaying similar levels of autistic traits (Baldwin and Costley, 2016). This, as I discuss in Chapter Five, means fewer autistic females are involved in research, 'leading to a vicious cycle of ignorance about possible gender differ-ences' (Fletcher-Watson and Happé, 2019, p.42).

I refer to female autistic research at various points within this book and present the vivid lived experiences of two autistic teenage girls alongside boys in Chapters Six to Eight in order to add to the limited body of research concerning females. Several recent texts focus primarily on autistic females and issues such as camouflaging and diagnosis (for example, Carpenter, Happé and Egerton, 2019).

Aetiology

In the 1960s Bettleheim (1967) facilitated the then widespread theory that autism originated from specific parenting styles, a belief subscribed to by Kanner, who is described as the main proponent of 'refrigerator mothers' (Stratheam, 2009). Jordan (1999, p.50) describes Kanner's belief that the 'mild autistic features of detachment and social difficulty that he saw in the parents of the children he treated could account for autism in their children'. Based on his own personal experiences, Bet-tleheim (1967) made the comparison between autistic children and those who suffered in the unloving and threatening conditions within Nazi concentration camps. It was thought the child developed autism as a result of a lack of warmth from parents, particularly mothers. From the 1970s, rejection of the theory of 'refrigerator mothering' grew as scientific research began uncovering a neurobiological basis for autism (Bernier and Gerdts, 2010). Prominent psychiatrists such as Sir Michael Rutter and Dr Susan Folstein (Folstein and Rutter, 1977) stu-died same-sexed twins (11 monozygotic and 10 dizygotic pairs) and concluded that autism is a genetically based disorder and not caused by poor parenting, or 'refrigerator mothering'. There has never been any scientific evidence that autism is caused by poor parenting.

The expanding body of genetic research has, and continues to, unveil the complexity of autism with multiple contributing genes. There are, as yet, no biological features providing a distinctive marker, or cause, of autism (Muhle et al., 2018). Importantly, there are no causal links between MMR vaccinations and autism, as purported by Dr Andrew Wakefield in 1998. This has been vehemently rejected (for instance, see

Modabbernia, Velthorst and Reichenberg, 2017). And Fletcher-Watson and Happé (2019, p.30) summarise that 'although we know autism has a genetic foundation, leading to neurobiological differences, it is diagnosed on the basis of a set of behaviours'.

Evolving images of ASD

In theory, research, policy and practice, autism is (more likely) viewed from the medical perspective 'as a situation of deficit compared to the norm of typical development' (Conn, 2014, p.14). This image is changing despite individuals having difficulties related to the dyad of challenges noted earlier; many of which are compounded by the social and sensory environments they are in. Those in the autism community are shaping their own identity rather than society doing it for them, with many autistic-advocates taking the position of self-determination and, as such, see the label as a badge of pride (Jordan, 2008; see Grandin, 2006).

On discussing the status of autism, Milton (2012) describes the use of three dominant psychological theories developed in the fields of neuroscience and psychology (theory of mind deficits, executive dysfunction and weak central coherence theory) which position autism as deficit, and deviant from the norm, augmenting the medical model of autism. When applied to education, autistic children, from the medical perspective, are undergoing a form of treatment to modify or change them – a pursuit of normalisation. As I revisit several times, there is a lack of research literature that explores the perspectives of autistic people, to challenge deficit mindsets. As such, 'autism is not just an invisible disability to many ... the autistic voice is made invisible in the current culture of how knowledge is produced about "autistic people"' (Milton, 2012, p.885).

It is commonly cited, and thought, that autistic people can have difficulties with empathy. In proposing the concept of a 'double empathy problem', Milton (2012) recognises that autistic people often lack empathy or insight into non-autistic perceptions and culture, but, equally, non-autistics also lack empathy into the minds and culture of autistic people. This can lead to difficulties experienced by some autistic young people being exacerbated; by, for example, a lack of autism understanding or willingness to adapt teaching approaches or research methodologies (see Chapters Two and Four). I have worked with several pupils who empathise so much with others that they intensely experience the feelings of the other person.

There are various definitions, perspectives and theories of autism (such as behavioural, biological and communicative/psychological – see

Fletcher-Watson and Happé, 2019). For instance, the neurodiversity movement, aligned to the social model of disability, conceptualises autism as a difference, with strengths to be celebrated, and not as a disorder to be cured. Spillers, Sensui and Linton (2014), from analysing online forum data from 76 autistic people, suggest that this neurodiversity movement seeks to remove stigma from autism: autism as inseparable from their identity. Autistic young people, in research by Humphrey and Lewis (2008a), also suggest that autism should be viewed as a difference as opposed to ongoing pathologising. The young people we hear from later in this book offer a range of perspectives; autism as a difference, autism as a characteristic (much like the colour of one's hair) and autism as problematic (see Chapter Eight). In short, the social model of autism, as with disability more widely, emphasises that difficulties are socially created and premised on the attitudes and actions of others (Conn, 2014; Conn, 2018d). As Fletcher-Watson and Happé (2019, p.148) discuss, 'social models of autism, and disability more generally, offer a positive way to conceptualise autism, important for public awareness and understanding'.

It is unsurprising, therefore, that autistic people afford less priority to causation research, in part due to the potential for resources to be redirected towards 'cause and cure' rather than resource services or research to help support autistic people (Baker, 2011; Pellicano and Stears, 2011). That said, the pursuit of biological explanation also helps discredit dangerous causation myths (such as links to vaccination or parenting style, noted earlier) and may allow the onset of support earlier in a person's life. Fletcher-Watson and Happé (2019) advocate that any biological discoveries should be embedded in a robust ethical framework so that findings are used for positive endeavour. However, it is also suggested that for some autistic people and their relatives that the cure movement, arguably opposing neurodiversity, is supported; the difficulties of autism on daily life are too great (Kapp et al., 2013).

Other models of disability and perspectives of autism have been suggested. For example, the affirmative model suggested by Swain and French (2000) combines aspects of both the medical and the social model. Core features of autism and the role played by social attitudes, such as those from teachers, are acknowledged as impacting on how a person experiences disability. I find this the most pragmatic way to conceptualise autism in order to best meet the child's needs in education. However, I am not convinced that the legislation and policies referred to in Chapter Two have found a balance between the medical and social models of disability. For me it is important to be mindful of both fields of thought, while being respectful to an individual's position on autism – only then can awareness be enhanced, understanding be developed and thus greater empathy be shown for those we educate and involve in research, which will, in turn, add to the autistic young person's sense of belonging and help support them to be themselves. The terminology we use matters.

Terminology

The language used to describe autism is currently the subject of debate (Fletcher-Watson and Happé, 2019). For instance, using terminology such as 'disorder' – still widely used – implies deficit, with the term Autism Spectrum Conditions (ASC) being more closely aligned to a social conceptualisation of special educational needs and disability (SEND). It implies 'difference' as opposed to 'deficit'. At present, identity-first language is preferred by a large proportion of the autism community (Kenny et al., 2016). Reflecting this, the term 'autistic young person' rather than 'young person with autism' has been adopted throughout this book. The latter would be awkward and would describe a person as marred with autism and suggest that autism is separate from who they are. Gernsbacher (2017) highlights that language can be stigmatising, particularly when different constructions are used to describe children with and without a disability. For example, the phrases 'typically developing child' and a 'child with autism' place the latter as 'less than' (Fletcher-Watson and Happé, 2019, p.ix; see also Pellicano et al., 2017). We should endeavour to use respectful language which does not stigmatise.

As with the linear connotations associated with the term 'spectrum', the use of terms such as 'low functioning' and 'high functioning' serves to create a 'one-or-other' concept of autism and of a person's capabilities. 'High functioning' may simply mean greater ability to mask, camouflage or compensate. Milton (2019, personal correspondence) highlights that the use of these terms narrows our focus on human beings in terms of 'functions'. Both, he said, could be considered demeaning stereotypes rather than addressing diversity and the uneven – or spiky – profile autistic young people often have. In essence, the term 'low functioning' can be seen to ignore a child's strengths and the term 'high functioning' can underplay or disregard the difficulties a person experiences and their need for support with, for example, sensory and social aspects of the school environment. Both can be offensive to many in the autism community. In reality, for many of the autistic young people I work with and those whom we hear from in this book, they could be described as high and low functioning depending on the circumstances and situations they are in. Their ability to communicate and interact with others depends on many variables, including the school environment, the social situation and, from experience, how their day has progressed up to that point. Their 'functioning' fluctuates, and much of this fluctuation stems from the understanding and support they experience – or do not experience (see Chapter Six). The determining factor, arguably, is whether or not the young person is within an autism-friendly school environment – this is also true of how we engage autistic people, whether child or adult, in research (an area explored in Chapter Five).

2   Inclusion

Introduction

In this chapter I present salient aspects of the educational inclusion debate. To contextualise the rest of the book, I explore issues such as 'what is inclusion?' and question the apparent shift from integration to inclusion (all of which are revisited in Chapter Eight). I outline the universalist and moderate perspectives of inclusion before considering how disability is conceptualised, how this can influence the involvement of children in research, and how they are supported in the classroom. In doing so I explore the shift from a medicalised model of disability to a social model, and the dilemma associated with (diagnostic) labelling to signify and support difference.

I end the chapter by outlining the Inclusive Pedagogical Approach and Universal Design for Learning as approaches that can help engender inclusive practice. I begin the chapter by providing a brief outline of the legislative framework within which schools and educators operate in the United Kingdom.

Legislative context

The Autism Act Northern Ireland (2011) recognises Autistic Spectrum Disorder as a disability. As with many other disabilities, not all autistic children have a learning difficulty or are deemed to have special educational needs (SEN), although, as I will explore, many face difficulties accessing learning and education – this is despite many being in mainstream (inclusive) education and therefore being considered 'mainstream able'.

In Northern Ireland (NI), the outgoing Code of Practice on the Identification and Assessment of Special Educational Needs (Department of Education for Northern Ireland [DENI], 1998, p.1) defines SEN as 'a learning difficulty which calls for special educational provision to be made'. A child has a learning difficulty when they have 'significantly greater difficulty in learning than the majority of children of his or her age, and/or has a disability which hinders his or her use of everyday educational facilities' (DENI, 1998, p.1). Thus, the special provision is different from, or in addition to, the regular provision made for children of a similar chronological age. This may include withdrawal support, additional adult assistance, or being educated in a special unit or special school.

The Department for Education Northern Ireland (2009) published 'Every School a Good School' (ESaGS) with a view to having a more comprehensive inclusive framework. This was delivered in the expectation of changing how diversity in special needs education was conceptualised by educational professionals. This document, adopted as a policy for school improvement in NI, states there is a 'wish to move away from the in-child deficit model to a much wider approach in which additional educational need is a concept in which SEN is an integral element' (p.7). Prior to this, the Special Educational Needs and Disability (NI) Order 2005 (SENDO) was enacted to enhance the rights of children with SEN to attend mainstream schools, giving due consideration to parental opinions. The Department of Education for Northern Ireland (2005, p.18) espoused that SENDO

> will strengthen the right of an ordinary school place for children with a Statement, unless it is against the wishes of parents, or it is incompatible with the efficient education of others.

More recently the Special Educational Needs and Disability (SEND) Act (Northern Ireland) (2016), as one part of the new SEN framework anticipated for implementation in 2019 (Department of Education, 2017), strengthens the duties of the Education Authority for NI (and schools) to support the needs of children with SEN and their parents. This Act, albeit still in its infancy and not fully implemented at the time of writing, remains focused on identification (or labelling) and early intervention, such as reducing the timeframe from 26 to 20 weeks for the assessment of SEN and allocation of a Statement of SEN. For comparison, in England the Children and Families Act (2014) mandates that children and young people are given Education, Health and Care Plans (ECHP) instead of Statements of SEN. ECHPs were introduced with the hope of transforming SEN support from that of fixed need and provision – as identified in Statements of SEN – to be about aspirations and outcomes.

The SEND Act (2016) extends the definition of the child in order to allow a young person who reaches 19 years of age to remain in school until the end of the school year and gives young people (who are not at the upper compulsory school age) the right to approach the SEND Tribunal with a SEN appeal or discrimination claim. It also places the child at the centre of the SEN assessment process, requiring the Education Authority to seek and apply due regard for the child's views on decisions that impact on them. However, the Act makes no provision for advocacy of this right (see Chapter Three), and 'it is yet to be seen whether children with disabilities will, in fact, have their views given due weight' (Goodall and MacKenzie, 2018, p.1662).

One of the most notable changes to the 1998 Code of Practice (CoP) is that statementing will be streamlined from a five-stage to a three-stage process. The new CoP and legislation stipulate that if a pupil is placed on the SEN register the school must provide additional SEN provision at Stage One (they must have a personal learning plan [PLP], formerly an individualised education plan [IEP]). This is strengthened by the Education Authority and/or the Health and Social Care Trust at Stage Two and then supported with a Statement of SEN at Stage Three. Up to this point, under the 1998 CoP, a child could be registered at Stage One on the school's SEN register without the need for a specific PLP or IEP.

Children and young people with a medical or physical diagnosis have historically been placed on Stage One under the 1998 CoP despite no additional special educational provision being required; they will now be placed on a medical register (see Figure 2.1 below).

Of particular note for autistic pupils is that they will be listed on a school's medical register with any associated SEN highlighted under the SEN register using, arguably, more descriptive SEN categories than those previously applied, such as 'emotional and wellbeing difficulties'. A pupil who is placed on the medical register without additional SEN may benefit from a school passport where associated reasonable adjustments are recorded. Aside from positioning autism squarely within the medical model (via the medical register), the suggestion that an autistic child could be required to carry a 'school passport' so as to trigger reasonable adjustments could prove counterproductive.

For instance, imagine a child in their first year of secondary school who is being supported with class-to-class transitioning. They are allowed to leave class slightly earlier than their peers to enable them to avoid the potential 'chaos of the corridor' (see Humphrey and Lewis, 2008a). A new or substitute teacher, with no working knowledge of the child, questions them about being on the corridor during lesson time.

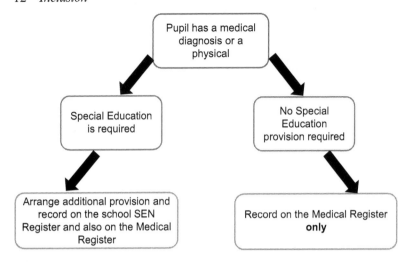

Figure 2.1 Recording procedures for the 2019 Code of Practice

This child, in what could then be an intense interaction for them, particularly as they are likely to be anxious and worried about getting to their next class before other pupils fill up the corridor, has then to produce the passport to *prove* that they have been permitted out early. I am not saying that the idea is ill-founded, it is a mechanism to indicate that adjustments be made for a child who has not been formally identified as having additional SEN (and can be used as a more pupil-centric support mechanism than an IEP), but caution is required when approaches like these are proposed. They may be adopted and applied indiscriminately and without flexibility as the 'what to do' approach without clear thought for each individual pupil.

Whilst the difficulties associated with inclusion are universal, in a jurisdiction such as the UK, which has devolved power to Scotland, NI and Wales, the range of difficulties, policies and practices differ, albeit that the 'prevailing policy discourse is of equality, inclusion and informed choice' (Chaney, 2012, p.28). For instance, 'Getting It Right for Every Child' (GIRFEC) (Scottish Government, 2013) states that children 'need to be safe, nurtured, healthy, achieving, active, respected, responsible and included' (Scottish Executive, 2006, p.4). In Northern Ireland, the 'Every Child an Equal Child' (Equality Commission for Northern Ireland, 2008, p.4), which is similar in sentiment to the GIRFEC, highlights that

> every child has equality of access to a quality educational experience; every child is given the opportunity to reach their potential;

and the ethos of every school promotes the inclusive participation of all children.

In reality, however, what is experienced by many may be more akin to integration than inclusion, while legislation is still focused on an 'identify and fix approach'.

What is inclusion? Searching for a definition

Educational inclusion is considered to be fractured and problematic, whose realisation is at the forefront of educational policy agendas in many countries (Pellicano, Bölte and Stahmer, 2018). It is open to wide interpretation by teachers, parents, educators and other stakeholders (Cigman, 2007). Imray and Colley (2017, p.1) state that 'inclusion has become a recurring trope of academic writing on education; it is trotted out as an eternal and unarguable truth, but it is neither.' Although I do not wish to walk along this well-trodden path for long, I do want to discuss some of the arguments in order to contextualise the insights and perspectives of autistic young people that I will present later. I argue that the pursuit of inclusion (mainstreaming) for all has failed, resulting in many autistic children becoming educational collateral damage, excluded by inclusion (an issue discussed towards the end of this chapter and later within the book). This is also the view of Hornby (2015, p.236), for instance, who states that it is

> now widely recognised that the policy of 'full inclusion', with its vision of all children being educated in mainstream classrooms for all or most of their time at school is impossible to achieve in practice'. (See Chapter Four)

Inclusion as a process, state, act and right (see Chapter Three) is described as a broadening agenda respecting diversity amongst all learners, irrespective of difference, disposition or disability (Artiles et al., 2006). Inclusion, further, is aimed at reducing educational and societal exclusion by 'celebrating difference' (Barton, 1998, p.231). It is also described as being 'crucial for participation in other function systems, such as economy and politics' (Michailakis and Reich, 2009, p.41). Inclusion, therefore, should be how all children are supported in fully participating in learning and in school life, and not be solely confined to SEN (Ainscow, 2014; Warnock, 2005). As will be discussed later, inclusion is part of a much larger picture than mere physical placement. Importantly, it should be recognised as a complex process and not a static state.

Despite the contested nature of inclusion, the underlying principles are that it should be driven by equality, social justice and children's rights, involving children learning together so that inclusion is founded upon empowerment, acceptance, equity and – as the young people we hear from later testify – belonging.

Equity, as a pillar of inclusion, should not be withheld because of disability (Rioux, 2014). However, it is important to recognise that in order to offer equity in education – and be inclusive – simply being in receipt of the same (equal) treatment does not always equate to equal opportunities to learn (De Valenzuela, 2014). For instance, placing an autistic child who has auditory processing difficulties in the mainstream classroom may be viewed as treating him equally – after all, they are within the same classroom as their peers. However, not adapting the language or approach used by the teacher, such as breaking learning into steps, providing processing time or offering visually supported instructions, fails to provide equity in opportunity for the autistic child to access the same lesson and learn (this is also applicable to research; see Chapter Five). If this is all that a child experiences – physical placement or, in other words, integration – then they in effect become excluded by misconceived notions of what inclusive education is. As the accounts of autistic young people reveal in Chapter Eight, inclusion should not be synonymised with mainstream, since mainstream education does not automatically result in inclusion.

I now discuss the *apparent* shift from integration to inclusion. I refer to several rights instruments in the next section, all of which are detailed in Chapter Three.

From integration to inclusion

The ubiquitous use of the term 'inclusion', particularly 'mainstream inclusion', often describes pedagogy which is, in reality, assimilationist, integrationist and at worst exclusionary, premised on the hope that normality will somehow 'rub off' onto disabled children (Michailakis and Reich, 2009). For instance, placing an autistic child in mainstream can be seen as inclusion, depending on an individual's perception, yet in reality may be nothing more than physical integration (Goodall, 2018a, p.2).

When the term 'inclusion' is wedded to 'mainstream education for all' then the transformation from integration to all children (or more, at least) experiencing inclusion is less likely to occur (see Rogers, 2007) – an aspect readily discussed by autistic young people in Chapter Eight. The Committee on the Rights of Persons with Disabilities outlines in General Comment 4 (GC4) on Article 24 (right to inclusive education) of the UNCRPD (United Nations, 2016) that, without accompanying structural changes to create an accessible built environment alongside modifications in teaching methods and approaches, placing children with disabilities in mainstream classes does not constitute inclusion. Paragraph 11 further asserts that 'integration does not automatically guarantee the transition from segregation to inclusion'. This is echoed in the Report of the Special Rapporteur on the right to education (United Nations, 2017, para.113), which indicates that states

> must ensure all children receive the special assistance they require to address their individual needs; they cannot simply be added to classrooms without accommodation.

Unfortunately, as Rioux (2014, p.134) suggests, the 'onus is often on the individual to fit within the system not on the system to fit the individual' – this is reflected by some of the young people we hear from later, and also by others I teach. Hodge, Rice and Reidy (2019, p.17) summarise the importance of systemic change and the impact of the lack thereof for autistic children, which in turn can contribute to a devalued sense of self (although this is not the case universally across education systems):

> School is understood to be a site of change and development but currently it is only the autistic pupils who are expected to mutate, or at least self-regulate, into something less autistic, whilst the disabling systems and structures of education may be observed and regretted but are, for the most part, left undisturbed.

Inclusion in practice

Academic agenda

As a greater range of abilities has to be accommodated, the inclusive agenda may be conceived as opposing drives for academic improvements, within which mainstream schools are entangled. One outcome of this is that autistic pupils and others with SEND can be seen as a resource burden and possible threat to school performance within an education culture of testing and examination, with standards measured on narrow academic criteria rather than how inclusive they are (Thomas and Loxley, 2007). This creates a competitive system whereby schools, subject departments, teachers and pupils are concerned with outcome data. It is reasonable to suggest that teachers and schools are more readily judged by the final output they get from pupils and not necessarily on the journey travelled by each – or, indeed, the commitment and support of their teacher(s). I would suggest that these efforts, and individual successes, are not being celebrated as they ought because they are overshadowed by the emphasis on (hard) quantitative data (such as school attendance or academic grades). Consequently, 'softer' measures of success (such as a child gaining in confidence) are less readily reflected within documentation, such as reports prepared by school inspectors.

However, when inclusion is conceived as more than physical integration and achievement is broadened to include social, emotional and physical development as fundamental enablers of academic improvement – and not premised only on examination results – then both can be improved and achieved (Florian and Rouse, 2001; Morewood, 2012). Without social and emotional wellbeing, qualifications will be difficult to utilise by the young person. Increasing academic achievement for all students is also viewed as a pillar of inclusion. Ainscow (2014) suggests the academic standards and inclusive agendas are intertwined.

Exclusion in inclusion

Warnock reignited the debate on the value of universal inclusion in 2005 when she described inclusion as disastrous, with the result that many children had become casualties of an ideology of 'all children under one roof' (Warnock, 2005, p.22). Warnock proposed then that we should include children in the 'common educational enterprise of learning wherever they can learn best' (p.39). I suggest that this is as pertinent today, if not more so. For example, small *specialist* schools, such as the Alternative Education Provision (AEP) in which I teach, could be described as inclusive for those children who feel excluded by attempts at mainstream inclusion (see Goodall, 2019) – and, as we will hear, the autistic young people do not want the term inclusion to be synonymous with mainstream school. Attempting to accommodate in one school all children with diverse needs, such as those with autism or complex emotional and behavioural difficulties, demonstrates the impracticalities of full inclusion for schools and the negative impact on young people themselves. However, this is not to say that we should not strive to ensure all mainstream schools are as autism-friendly, or as inclusive, as possible (see Goodall, 2015a). Again, seeking the views, experiences and thoughts of those insiders – the young people – for whom our education system should serve will help realise this.

Inclusion, as it exists, is often a facade for a system of 'selective exclusion', whereby children are excluded from various aspects and functions of the educational macrosystem (Michailakis and Reich, 2009) – albeit inadvertently at times (see Chapter Six). Inclusion, and indeed exclusion, occur at three levels: societal, organisational and interactional (between individuals). Rogers (2007, p.63) suggests exclusion also occurs practically, by being withdrawn from class for individual support (although, as I suggest later, this depends on the nature of the individual support); intellectually, by being disadvantaged in accessing the curriculum and assessment in the same way as peers, and emotionally; and by having reduced social networks based on difficulties in interacting deeply with peers.

Warnock (2005) argues that a body of evidence exists to indicate that rejection, teasing and exclusion are experienced by children with SEN in mainstream schools (such as autistic children). As will be explored in Chapters Six and Nine, mainstream inclusion can result in educational, social and emotional exclusion for autistic children and young people (see Goodall, 2015b). Warnock (2005, p.43) also suggested that inclusion is 'experienced as a painful kind of exclusion', with children often being physically included (or integrated) but emotionally excluded. 'They suffer all the pains of the permanent outsider'. For instance, the bustling, somewhat unpredictable social and sensory mainstream environment is at odds with the needs of many autistic young people. And not questioning the 'illusionary' ideology of full inclusion may indeed be deleterious to those pupils it should serve (Michailakis and Reich, 2009, p.41). This, as Slee (2011) contends, is the challenge for inclusive education: to avoid the continued repetition of exclusion – whether formally or informally – in mainstream classrooms. Noteworthy is the recent 'Timpson review of school exclusion' (Timpson, 2019), which asserts 'we must also take the necessary steps to ensure exclusion from school does not mean exclusion from education, so that all children are getting the education they deserve'. This review advocates for the use of alternative provision (such as the AEP where I teach) as a positive new start; albeit it outlines wide variation in the quality and breadth of this provision (see also Goodall, 2019).

Universal, or moderate inclusion?

Universal, or full, inclusionists are guided by the premise of possibility; the possibility that inclusion in mainstream school will support every child irrespective of circumstance, SEN or disability (Cigman, 2007). Universalists promote full inclusion as the ideal scenario, as one reflecting the society of which we would like to be part (Lauchlan and Greig, 2015). Universalists accept, however, that mainstream does not yet cater for all children with SEN or disability (SEND) (Cigman, 2010), but assert that it is a process of learning from mistakes, rather than accepting that full inclusion is not possible. Universalists, further, are reluctant to conceptualise individual difference according to the medical model (see below). They align special schools to deficit conceptions of SEN, and consider this type of provision as exclusionary, demeaning and humiliating (Centre for Studies in Inclusive Education [CSIE], 2004). Full inclusion contrasts with the realities of what is possible in schools, that a wide range of needs, but not all, can be supported with correctly designed environments, resource allocation, training and supportive attitudes.

As a moderate inclusionist I acknowledge that individual difference is important for supporting need and respecting a person's individuality, but recognise that mainstream education should be the aim only when it can effectively support the child (see Warnock, 2005). I have worked with many young people who are 'given a go' in mainstream secondary education in the hope that they will somehow manage to cope, even while their classroom assistance is reduced (or removed) when they move to secondary education in what is then a setting which poses more challenges. This often results in missing several months of education prior to being referred to the AEP in which I teach (1 discuss the greater difficulties experienced by autistic young people in secondary-level education in Chapter Four).

Moderate inclusionists see a role for individual and parental choice in where children with SEND should be educated, valuing the appropriate and sensitive use of labels to help children access effective education, where the child feels they would best belong, that is planned and resourced to match the diversity of need.

Despite these different positions on the extent to which inclusion can be realised by mainstream provision, most will argue for the values of inclusion. The fundamental value of meeting the needs and maximising the potential of every child is shared by all who support educational inclusion to whatever degree (Cigman, 2010); but children for whom mainstream inclusion is not enabling should not be treated as a means to other people's ends (Cigman, 2007). Using those children who will 'inevitably miss out on an education in mainstream, however inclusively orientated', is to pursue a utopian ideal of 'inclusion for all' in one school without being cognisant of the impact it has on many children (Cigman, 2010, p.160).

I have briefly outlined two perspectives on the extent to which inclusion should be enacted: the universalist perspective, aligned to a rights-based approach to inclusion which, as discussed in Chapter

Three, advocates the right to an inclusive education for all; and the moderate inclusionist perspective, aligned to a 'needs-based' approach, whereby mainstream school is one setting within a range of provision available to educate young people with SEN and disabilities based on the needs of the child (this includes special[ist] schools and units within mainstream settings). The inclusion discourse often appears diametrically opposed, with mainstream education positioned against specialist or non-mainstream provision. To reconcile this, Hornby (2015) discusses the middle ground and suggests that we should speak of inclusive special education to synthesise the concepts of inclusion and special education:

> The definition of inclusive special education encompasses a synthesis of the philosophies and practices of both inclusive education and special education. It involves educating children with SEND in the most inclusive settings in which their special educational needs can be met effectively, using the most effective instructional strategies, with the overarching goal of facilitating the highest level of inclusion in society post school for all young people with SEND (Hornby, 2015, p.239).

In the next two sections I outline the apparent shift from a medical model to a social model of disability and also consider the dilemma associated with diagnostic labels. How disability is conceived and the value and attitudes applied to diagnostic labels by teachers (and peers) underpin how inclusion is conceptualised and enacted in practice (including how we involve autistic young people in research).

From a medical to a social model of disability

The medical model focuses on in-child impairments and conceives of disability as a personal tragedy (Oliver, 1996). The child is considered deficient, having a pathological problem requiring a diagnosis which can, possibly and hopefully, be fixed. This can perpetuate deterministic notions that a child's ability is static and non-transformable, and that disability and SEN are constant across all contexts (Spratt, Florian and Rouse, 2010). Oliver (1990) argues that thinking needs to shift from within the deficit model of viewing disability as the inevitable outcome of personal impairment to understanding the socially constructed nature of disability, regularly cited as the 'social model' of disability, and an aspect of the Inclusive Pedagogical Approach presented at the end of this chapter.

The social model locates the problem within the person-environment relationship: it is the failure of society (and schools) to recognise and accommodate a person's needs by removing environmental and attitudinal barriers. Barnes (2012, p.12) summarises the social model by stating that 'impairment may be a human constant but "disability" need not and should not be'. Ekins (2015, p.275) contends that for schools to move towards a more inclusive social model there needs to be an emphasis on individual approaches, alongside removing barriers to learning and participation, which involve the pupil in discussions and progress reviews. The latter point on participation, and the involvement of young people in decisions that impact them and in them having their voices heard and given due weight, is developed further when I discuss children's rights in Chapter Three.

Arguably, the inclusion agenda has shifted attention from attempting to rectify 'within-child' deficits (medical model) to social constructions of disability (social model). However, although modifications can be made to the social and physical environment within which a child is placed, 'one cannot eliminate the individual dimension altogether' (Low, 2007, p.9). Therefore individual characteristics should be considered by teachers and policymakers if the needs of all children are to be met – as the legislation referred to at the start of this chapter stipulates that we do. And, as I present later, researchers should also be minded to support any personal needs, such as communication preferences. If biological characteristics remain the singular focus, learning difficulties and SEND may continue to be viewed as individual deficits; schools and individual educators are let 'off the hook' as 'faults' remain solely within the child. If, on the other hand, the social environment is seen as the primary contributory cause of disability, we will overlook bona fide medical causes of disability. Oliver (1996) suggests that only by focusing on the social model of disability can educators deny a person's experiences of their own body. That said, viewing disability from the perspective of the social model can compel educators and researchers alike to search for reasons why the child is not progressing in education as would be expected.

To reconcile this, Warnock (2005) suggests that the SEN framework should move beyond individualised medical labels to consider other socio-cultural factors. These factors include community and parental attitudes to inclusion, funding allocation, curriculum and teaching methods. For autistic young people, as will be discussed, the interaction of both in-child and environmental factors, such as teacher understanding, can enable or hinder inclusion. From professional experience, and as suggested under the legislative context section earlier, the education system within which we operate in the UK (particularly in NI) is still positioned within the medical model. The mechanisms used to *help* children receive legally recognised and protected resource allocation pivot on a Statement of special educational need; these documents focus heavily on a child's deficits. Children are classified first and foremost as challenges to be overcome, with their strengths taking second place to their deficits. Yet without a diagnostic label or a Statement of SEN (or other such mechanism, such as the EHCP) the approaches used, the learning environment offered, the supportive structures needed and possible judgements made about a child by educators may be antithetical to their needs.

I now briefly discuss the use of diagnostic labels and the positive and negative implications of identifying difference between children and young people in this way. I highlight the potential pitfalls if we, as educators and researchers, do not consider each autistic child as an individual, despite their shared diagnostic label. However, as I discuss in the next section, I am mindful that as researchers we often purposefully co-opt or exclude potential research participants based on these diagnostic labels.

Labelling and difference

Without a formal diagnostic label, children may not be able to avail of additional resources (Hornby, 2012). It is unsurprising, therefore, that diagnoses are on the rise to unlock support and services (Hollenweger, 2014). For example, recent pressure on the Northern Ireland Executive (the devolved government of NI) for expeditious ASD diagnostic services and more educational resources, via a petition from more than 8,000 parents and professionals, resulted in an allocation of £2m of funding (see UTV News, 2016). This exemplifies a system that requires parents to battle to have their children formally diagnosed in order to access resources to help their child access education and cope within mainstream school (such as being supported by a classroom assistant). Diagnostic and post-diagnosis support and provision across a relatively small province such as NI will depend on one's postcode (and across the UK). In NI there seems to be a system where diagnostic services are improving and waiting times are reducing, but – and with great importance to education – the expedited diagnostic process is not yet adequately matched by post-diagnosis support.

Labels, however, can bring benefits other than resources. From discussions with autistic people it is evident that a diagnosis helps explain, and brings recognition of, who they are, removing the feeling of identity uncertainty. Perhaps this is why, as discussed in Chapter One, the autistic community prefers identity-first language signifying their belonging to the autistic community (Kenny et al., 2016).

However, diagnostic labels are not neutral or value-free. Diagnostic labelling can reduce the individual's sense of self, and how they are perceived by others, to a diagnostic category – 'framed as disordered' (Hodge, Rice and Reidy, 2019, p.2) – rather than being valued as a person. This can 'open the door' for ablest practices, described by Levi (2005, p.1) as 'prejudicial attitudes and discriminatory behaviours towards persons with a disability'. These can in turn 'promote unequal treatment because of apparent or assumed physical, mental or behavioural differences' (Terry, 1996, pp.4–5). With regards to autism, homogenising young people because of shared diagnoses can result in ableism. Hodge, Rice and Reidy (2019) propose a framework to help challenge ableist practices, including recognition and celebration of the contributions made by autistic pupils even when these are not made in typical or expected forms.

For me, labels are umbrella terms that denote common characteristics, challenges or differences amongst children but which can undermine the strengths a person may have by being over-simplistic or by using terminology tendentiously. For instance, the still widely used but increasingly criticised term 'Low Functioning Autism' implies a lack of capacity (Kenny et al., 2016). Depending on the connotations associated with a label, perhaps originating from a teacher's past experiences, children may be stigmatised as difficult (by prejudicial attitudes noted above), thus creating a hierarchy and an 'intractable cycle' (Florian, 2014b) whereby children are automatically stigmatised as problematic before a teacher tries to build a relationship with them. This may underscore why autistic children have been largely missing in educational research (see Chapter Five). Evans and Lunt (2002) note that children with physical difficulties or moderate learning difficulties are deemed easy to include, while children with emotional and behavioural difficulties, severe learning difficulties or autism are classed by teachers as most difficult to include (see also Humphrey and Symes, 2013). This perspective may, in part, underpin the higher educational exclusion rates for autistic young people discussed further in Chapter Four.

Also, sometimes one part of a term overshadows the other – such as 'behavioural' in the term 'social, emotional and behavioural difficulties' (SEBD), although, in NI under the SEND Act (2016), this term will transition to the broad category 'social, behavioural, emotional and wellbeing' with sub-categories based on external assessment (social and behavioural difficulties; emotional and wellbeing difficulties; and 'severe challenging behaviour associated with severe learning difficulties [SLD] and/or profound and multiple learning difficulties [PMLD]').

Importantly, the label is not necessarily the barrier to inclusion; rather it is that the attitude or perception a teacher (or peer) has about children who share a particular diagnostic label can limit inclusion in education (and also in research). Utilising a (diagnostic) label for a child's long-term benefit requires that they are not defined, misunderstood or indeed stereotyped by their diagnosis. Treweek et al. (2018) found three emergent themes when exploring stereotypes with a group of 12 autistic adults (aged 20–63 years). These are being described as weird, that stereotypes had negative consequences for them and that they feel autistic people are viewed as a homogenous group. By listening to, and seeking advice from, young people themselves we can develop our understanding of how diverse autism is.

Homogenising a child can result in their individuality being lost, leading to the inflexible use of approaches to support each individual, just because that is 'what is done' for autistic children so it must be indiscriminately done for all. Strategies are often incorrectly advocated on a 'one size fits all' premise (Kucharczyk et al., 2015; Ruble, Dalrymple and McGrew, 2010), which, from experience, can stifle progress and cause undue frustration for the young person. I want to end this sub-section with an analogy, which helps me visualise and explain a framework for supporting autistic young people in education (and research).

Take a pizza. Imagine the base as the strong foundation of understanding, autism-acceptance and a willingness to support autistic young people in the school ethos and policy. The sauce represents creating an environment which is as autism-friendly as possible (such as adapting the geographical and sensory aspects of the school), having classrooms with clear areas of transition, use of natural light (no fluorescent lights), having safe spaces to use to de-stress and where pedagogy is flexible, or, with regard to research, ensuring the research environment is suitable. The toppings represent various strategies for individual young people – just like pizza toppings, some children may 'like' the same thing and that is okay, but various combinations may be needed for different autistic children within one class or school. Toppings, or strategies, may need to be changed or tried in different combinations to find what works. Crucially the base and sauce remain in place while different strategies, or toppings, are tried to find what works best. And, from time to time, more of one strategy, or topping, may need to be added or additional ones required. Regarding research, this can be taken to mean providing a range of methods for supporting young people in sharing their experiences (see Chapter Five). Without such, inclusion through belonging, equity, empowerment and fairness is unlikely to be experienced.

Concluding comments

To this point, inclusive education has been discussed (mainly) from a theoretical perspective.

The Inclusive Pedagogical Approach (IPA) can help address the fractured nature of inclusion. This approach is underpinned by three assumptions: that teachers believe they are capable of teaching a diverse range of children (and that children have the capacity to learn); that they adapt practice in creative (and flexible) ways to support the learning of all children; and that they recognise difference as a fundamental aspect of development (Florian, 2014a).

Teachers are recognised as agents of change who can reduce educational inequality and influence outcomes for young people through non-deterministic conceptions of ability by recognising the transformable nature of each young person's capacity – described as 'learning without limits' (Hart et al., 2004). By considering the difficulties experienced by young people as challenges to be overcome, rather than deficits within the child, and thus aligning to a social construction of disability, change can continue to occur. Although, to caveat this, the policy within which we operate should espouse this.

To add to the 'labelling and difference' sub-section above, the 'what' and 'how' of learning supersedes the importance of a specific SEN label. It is what teachers choose to do (or not do) that can affect any child's capacity to learn (Spratt and Florian, 2015), such as building relationships with the children they teach, founded on an understanding and respect for who they are. The choices teachers make about teaching and learning, the strategies they use to provide an accessible curriculum through flexible pedagogy and the attitudes they hold signal much more than the content of the lesson taking place – they impact on the extent to which the micro level of the classroom and the macro level of the school can be experienced as inclusive (and autism-friendly). This ultimately impacts on the inclusivity of a classroom and school. Learning is limited (for all) if approaches remain inflexible and deterministic (Hart et al., 2004).

Fundamentally, an IPA challenges deterministic attitudes and practices to which contemporary mainstream education is (mostly) wedded. Practices such as ability grouping, streaming and 'separate' SEN provision are described by Spratt and Florian (2015, p.90) as structures 'which exacerbate difference by providing for some individuals or groups in ways that mark out and reinforce division'. For me, however, direct support and intervention can aid mainstream inclusion and individual or small-group support, such as social skills programmes, and should not automatically be mistaken for a medicalised 'need-to-fix' approach. Such interventions often aim to support children in understanding their personal needs, develop skills and build on their strengths to develop strategies that they can then transfer to the classroom environment, such as strategies to aid social interaction and manage anxiety, stress or emotional regulation.

Hart and Drummond (2014) describe ability grouping as a practice that confines teaching and learning; a child's ability and supposition for future achievement is perceived as limited, and arguably non-transformable. To overcome this, Morewood, Humphrey and Symes (2011) – who discuss making mainstream work for autistic children – advocate creating teaching groups based on personal needs (such as requiring more structure within an activity) and not ability within the given subject.

Like the IPA, Universal Design for Learning (UDL) is another pedagogical model for enabling curriculum access for all children through flexible and accessible learning environments (Rose, Gravel and Gordan, 2014). From this perspective, disability does not reside within the individual but in a curriculum which is unsupportive of, and inflexible to, a diverse range of abilities. Attitudinal change is of concern for both models.

Building on strengths and eradicating difficulties require an accessible pedagogical approach (Rose, Gravel and Gordan, 2014). It emphasises that a greater range of needs can be supported within the diverse classroom when practice is premised on the UDL principles of: multiple means of representation (what we learn); expression (how we learn); and engagement (why we learn). Providing greater support ensures high standards are preserved, whereby difference is not denied but is rejected as 'an excuse for inaction or exclusion' (Rioux, 2014, p.143). This underpins creating autism-friendly, more-inclusive schools for more learners by recognising that children respond differently to the general curriculum, depending on the social and sensory environment at the time. As approaches, both have transferrable principles for research.

In Chapter Three, inclusion will be considered from a children's rights perspective. And, as will be discussed across the remaining chapters, multiple factors impact on a school's accessibility, autism-friendliness, and, ultimately, the inclusivity of the setting (see Goodall, 2015a). As you will hear, the educational experiences, and in particular how autistic young people conceptualise inclusion, go 'against the grain' of inclusion agendas as laid down within legislation and championed by rights instruments such as Article 24 of the UNCRPD.

3 Rights perspective

Introduction

How children are perceived in society, and their place within research, is underpinned by the importance placed on them as rights holders. The rights of children, particularly those with SEND, are not always upheld in accordance with rights legislation. In this chapter I present a brief synopsis of children as rights holders and outline key international developments and rights instruments which have led to, and continue to advocate for, the right to inclusive education for all. I concentrate mainly on the United Nations Convention on the Rights of the Child (United Nations, 1989) and the United Nations Convention on the Rights of Persons with Disabilities (United Nations, 2006a). Together these conventions provide for autistic young people, their education and their place within research. The right to education, and in particular the right to inclusive education, becomes the focus of discussion.

Children as rights holders

Children's rights are 'a bespoke set of human rights' encompassing civil, political, social, economic and cultural rights (Lundy and Stalford, 2013, p.443). A significant difference between children's rights and those of adults is that 'due weight' should be afforded to children's views, an issue explored later. Importantly, rights are not gifts conditional upon the benevolence of others. They cannot be dissolved because it would be better for others if rights did not exist, which unfortunately is the reality for many children, particularly with SEND.

No one theory captures the complexity of rights. For instance, 'choice', or 'will', theory is founded upon the concept of children having the capacity to choose whether or not to exercise rights. From this theoretical position children cannot be described as rights holders if they lack the capacity to choose (Fortin, 2009). 'Interest', or 'welfare', theory recognises that children may not be capable of exercising their rights independently and must, therefore, have their interests or rights protected by duties, or obligations, imposed on others (Bainham and Gilmore, 2013). However, this surrogate approach could disempower children and reinforce notions of incompetency and dependency, which then permit 'adults to claim they are protecting children when the choices made may better serve adult interests' (Federle, 2009, p.324). For me, this underscores the paramount importance of seeking the voices of autistic young people about their education to ensure that 'decision-makers' are guided by the experts – the young people – and not by ideological crusades.

Some children, such as those with SEND, may be perceived as lacking the capacity to hold or exercise rights (see Byrne, 2019), especially in sharing their lived experiences in research or as decision-makers in their own lives. If capacity is used as a gauge for exercising rights, children are at the mercy of adults' goodwill as they cannot 'redefine themselves as competent beings' (Federle, 1994, p.344). Irrespective of their perceived competence, children of all ages have useful insights on matters that are important to them, such as how their education has been and how they would like it to be.

Children's rights protect three hierarchical categories of interest: essentials of care from parents and developmental and autonomy interests (Eekelaar, 1986; 2007). The UN Convention on the Rights of the Child, discussed below, added participatory rights to the international rights landscape. These rights encourage children to be valuable contributors to society and matters impacting on their lives, such as education.

United Nations Convention on the Rights of the Child (UNCRC)

The UNCRC (United Nations, 1989) was ratified by the United Kingdom in 1991. It has received international acclaim and was described early on as 'laying the foundation for a better world' (Eekelaar, 1992, p.234). Freeman (2012) suggests that children are dually recognised as 'becomings' on the journey to adulthood (Article 3, best interests) and as 'beings' (Article 12), as persons in their own right. They are social actors with agency who derive their own meaning, truth and opinion and construct authentic perspectives on matters that impact on them (Freeman, 2012). Hanson (2017) suggests, however, that we should move away from a binary model of childhood composed of the present and future child – as 'beings' and 'becomings' – and give due consideration to the past, and the child's lived experiences, by also recognising the child as a 'been'.

Rights help redress the power imbalance between adults and children to ensure 'rights flow downhill' to the powerless, thus affording children power and respect regardless of capacity (Federle, 1994). I will revisit power imbalance in Chapter Five when I consider core principles of participatory research with autistic children. Although acknowledging children's evolving capacity, albeit without defining capacity, the UNCRC is considered weak regarding disabled children, with Byrne (2012) suggesting it is aligned to a deficit medicalised perspective. Article 2, the non-discrimination provision, applies to children with disability, while Article 23(1) states that the disabled should 'enjoy a full and decent life', in conditions which facilitate the 'child's active participation in the community'.

And, as with all rights frameworks, the UNCRC is awash with qualifications concerned with resources. Caveats such as the care provided is 'subject to available resources' (within Article 23) exemplify the insufficiency of the UNCRC in affirming the rights of disabled children. However, the United Nations Committee on the Rights of the Child (United Nations, 1997, para.334) asserts that children with disabilities (such as autism) should not have rights doubly denied by being disabled and by being a child.

Exploring Article 12

Article 12 lies at the core of implementing all children's rights. It is described as 'an important principle and one that has certainly influenced the behaviour of many researchers' (Rose and Shevlin, 2017, p.68). Article 12 reads:

> 1. States Parties shall assure to the child who is capable of forming his or her own views the right to express those views freely in all matters affecting the child, the views of the child being given due weight in accordance with the age and maturity of the child.
> 2. For this purpose, the child shall in particular be provided the opportunity to be heard in any judicial and administrative proceedings affecting the child, either directly, or through a representative or an appropriate body, in a manner consistent with the procedural rules of national law (United Nations, 1989).

This right should be integral to decisions affecting children's lives. Duty bearers, such as teachers and policymakers, should support children in exercising this right to amplify, and not silence, their voices. In essence, it removes the focus from children as objects (of research) to people with a voice and places the onus on schools (and researchers) to presume that children have the capacity to form their own views (United Nations, 2009).

The use of the 'assure' ought to eradicate doubt and remove leeway for 'states parties' to exercise discretion in supporting children to express their views (UNCRC/C/GC/12, United Nations 2009, p.8). However, the impact of Article 12 is potentially diminished by being represented by simplistic phrases such as 'the voice of the child' and 'the right to participate' (Lundy, 2007). A progressive model (Figure 3.1) proposed by Lundy (2007), and revisited in Chapter Five, magnifies understanding beyond these phrases and demonstrates the complexity that the above phrases do not convey. Lundy's model considers four interconnected factors: voice (facilitated to form a view); space (opportunity to express a view); audience (to be listened to); and influence (views to be taken seriously and acted upon, as appropriate).

Excessive focus has been applied to Article 12 in isolation of other participation rights, interconnected Articles and principles as conceptualised in Figure 3.1. Without considering Article 12 in conjunction with other rights (and instruments, such as the UN Convention on the Rights of the Child) the complexity and importance of children's voices in research and matters which impact on them in education are diluted. In summary, Article 12 should be seen as interdependent with and indivisible from the remaining participation rights (Articles 13–17) and in conjunction with the other overriding principles of the UNCRC;

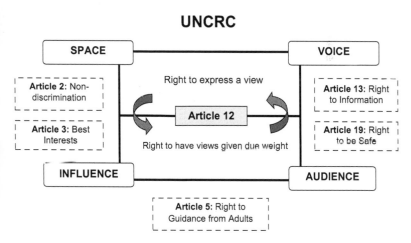

Figure 3.1 Conceptualising Article 12 from Lundy
Source: 2007, p.932

non-discrimination (Article 2), best interests (Article 3), right to guidance from adults (Article 5), and the right to be safe (Article 19) – all of which underpin ethical, inclusive rights-based participatory research (see Chapter Five).

United Nations Convention on the Rights of Persons with Disabilities (UNCRPD)

Although neither the UNCRC nor UNCRPD were drafted by children, the UNCRPD is the first rights instrument that places 'the spotlight firmly upon the breadth and depth of exclusionary and oppressive practices experienced by people with disabilities' (Byrne, 2012, p.419). It provides clarity and recognition that existing human and civil rights apply equally to disabled people, stating that they should have 'equal enjoyment of all human rights' (Article 1). It contains the obligation to apply 'due weight' to the views of children, as stipulated by the UNCRC, and recognises those with disabilities as social beings. Byrne (2012, p.421) suggests that the UNCRPD departs from a deficit becomings model which views children with disabilities as 'seemingly bereft of capacity and agency such that they can neither be "cured" nor "grow up"'. The UNCRPD brings a human rights dimension to disability and shifts focus from the medical to the social model of disability.

The UNCRPD Preamble emphasises disability as an 'evolving concept' emerging from 'the interaction between persons with impairments and attitudinal and environmental barriers' (United Nations, 2006). Article 7 of the UNCRPD (children with disabilities) provides further for the rights laid down in Article 12, namely the obligation that due weight should also be applied to the views of children with disabilities. However, that right has rarely been exercised (Lundy, 2018). Article 7 reads:

> 1. States Parties shall take all necessary measures to ensure the full enjoyment by children with disabilities of all human rights and fundamental freedoms on an equal basis with other children.
> 2. In all actions concerning children with disabilities, the best interests of the child shall be a primary consideration.
> 3. States Parties shall ensure that children with disabilities have the right to express their views freely on all matters affecting them, their views being given due weight in accordance with their age and maturity, on an equal basis with other children, and to be provided with disability and age-appropriate assistance to realize that right (United Nations, 2006a).

Point three holds particular importance when involving autistic young people in research. They should be supported in realising their right to express their views and have them given due weight. As it stands, their voices are sparse in the extant literature (see Chapter Five).

Right to education

This right has been a consistent feature since the UN was established. Article 13 of the International Covenant on Economic, Social and Cultural Rights (1966) obligates ratifying states to provide free elementary education widely and devise various forms of secondary education. The UK Human Rights Act (1998) incorporates the European Convention on Human Rights (1950) into domestic law, with Article 2(1) of the first protocol of the ECHR stating that 'no person shall be denied the right to education'. Lundy (2006, p.339) explains that education 'is the only Human Right which is administered compulsorily'; this combines rights to, in and through education.

UN General Comment No. 1 (2001) emphasises the interrelationship of the UNCRC provision by stating that Article 29(1) of the UNCRC enjoins governments to provide access to education (Article 28) and promotes the holistic development of the child. Article 29(1) stipulates that 'States parties agree that the education of the child shall be directed to: (a) the development of the child's personality, talents and mental and physical abilities to their fullest potential'.

If children are denied this substantive right to education – a 'multiplier of rights' (Tomaševski, 2001a, para.11) – they will struggle to realise other rights. Children's participation, as will be discussed in Chapter Five, is crucial to the realisation of their rights *through* education. As Tomaševski (2001b) suggests, rights are not just about accessing education; rights must be respected and assured within education, in a school where children feel safe, listened to and valued, and in one that develops the child holistically through curriculum delivery that is supportive of the child through the use of strategies that facilitate access to learning on an basis equal to their peers.

Right to inclusive education

Inclusive education is increasingly advocated by international declarations and instruments (UNESCO, 2009). UNCRC Article 23(1) and (3) alludes to the concept of inclusion, stating that children should achieve the fullest possible 'social integration' and active participation in the community. However, no specific reference is made to educating children with disabilities alongside mainstream peers (Freeman, 2000).

The Salamanca Statement (UNESCO, 1994) is described as the turning point when integration was replaced by a focus on inclusion (see Chapter Two). The statement provided that 'those with special educational needs must have access to regular schools which should accommodate them within a child-centred pedagogy capable of meeting their needs' (para.2). It further asked states 'to adopt as a matter of law or policy the principle of inclusive education, enrolling all children in regular schools, unless there are compelling reasons for doing otherwise' (para.3).

In summary, this statement, and framework for action on SEN, advocates that all children have the right to education and that children with SEN should be educated in regular mainstream schools that have a child-centred pedagogy. However, in stating that inclusion should provide 'effective education to the majority of children' (UNESCO, 1994, p.ix), the term 'majority' may be an acknowledgement that mainstream schools are not always able to cater for every child's need, such as those with complex medical or behavioural needs, or, as will be discussed in more detail in Chapter Four, many autistic children. The Salamanca Statement failed to provide a definition of inclusive education.

The Committee on the Rights of the Child General Comment No. 9 (United Nations, 2006b) specifically advocates inclusive education as the goal for educating children with disabilities and states that governments should aim to provide 'schools with appropriate accommodation and individual support' for children with disabilities. Thereafter, the UNCRPD then called on state parties to 'ensure an inclusive education system at all levels' (Article 24(1)), with the Committee on the Rights of the Child repeatedly emphasising that children need to be educated in mainstream settings (Byrne, 2019; Lundy, 2012). Disagreements did, however, exist in drafting of the UNCRPD about whether or not special education still had to be an option (Byrne, 2013; De Beco, 2014). For instance, draft Article 17 (3) provided that 'where the general education system does not adequately meet the needs of persons with disabilities special and alternative forms of learning should be made available ... (c) allow a free and informed choice between general and special systems' – noteworthy is that the young people we hear from in Chapter Eight align more to draft Article 17 than to codified Article 24. However, De Beco (2016) contends that the UNCRPD fails to clarify how inclusive education is to be implemented.

General Comment 4 (GC4) on Article 24 of the UNCRPD (United Nations, 2016, para.9) provides clarity.

> The right to inclusive education encompasses a transformation in culture, policy and practice in all ... educational environments to accommodate differing requirements and identities of individual

students, together with a commitment to remove barriers that impede that possibility.

Referring again to the Special Rapporteur on the Right to Education, this time the Right to Education of Persons with Disabilities (United Nations, 2007, para.50), it states 'the system that excludes cannot be the same system that includes or promises to include'. The antithesis of this is the lived reality for those young people we hear from later; the mainstream school – that which is often automatically heralded as inclusive – is not what is experienced by every child. Extensive attention is paid to the need for structural, cultural and attitudinal (value) changes in GC4. GC4 elaborates further on how inclusive education should be enacted (United Nations, 2016), as summarised in Goodall and MacKenzie (2018, pp.1662–1663):

> Inclusive education is to be understood as a 'fundamental right of all learners' at all levels (10a), which values 'the well-being of all students' and 'respects their inherent dignity and autonomy' (10b); and is a process of 'continuing and pro-active commitment to eliminate barriers impeding the right to education' (10d). 'Inclusion is a process that involves: systemic reform embodying changes and modifications in content, teaching methods, approaches, structures and strategies in education to overcome barriers ... to provide all students ... with an equitable and participatory learning experience and the environment that best corresponds to their requirements and preferences' (GC4, para.11).

As GC4 states, placing pupils with disabilities within mainstream classes without changes to, for example, organisation or curriculum and teaching and learning strategies does not constitute inclusion. An inclusive environment is one which embodies a number of core features. For example: a 'whole systems' approach by which resources should be invested to advance inclusive education (12a); a 'whole person' approach which recognises the capacity of every person to learn (c); respect for and value of diversity (e); and a 'learning friendly environment' where everyone feels safe and valued (f). Teachers, too, should receive education and training to provide them with the values and competencies to 'accommodate inclusive environments' (d).

Is the right to inclusive education right?

The Committee on the Rights of the Child has 'become increasingly critical' of educational provision for the child with disabilities and 'has developed an understanding of the right to education as one of inclusive education' (Byrne, 2019, p.39). However, inclusive education, if wedded to the concept of mainstreaming for all, without due regard for the individual child and how inclusive the individual mainstream school actually is or will be, brings into question whether placement within mainstream is what is right, morally, for that child and in their best interests. That is not to say that the right to inclusive education is not right, it is; but whether the child should be in mainstream school should be questioned with their best interests in mind. What is in the child's best interests in education is not defined in the UNCRC. The fact that it is broad and vague in nature makes it difficult to monitor its application, with the result that 'this principle has the potential to mean all things to all people' (Lundy and Kilkelly, 2006, p.336) and implementation varies considerably across different areas, such as education.

To add further complexity, UNCRC Article 3(1) and UNCRPD Article 7(2) use the indefinite article 'a' instead of the definite article 'the', and in doing so dilute the paramount principle by making the best interest of the child 'a' primary consideration, not 'the' primary consideration. Without exploring the child's opinions (as discussed in later chapters) it is impossible to arrive at a decision about what is in the child's best interest – demonstrating that Articles 3 and 12 of the UNCRC complement one another (United Nations, 2009, paras.71 and 74). The child's best interest is often limited to the adult perspective, but we must not forget that 'adults are the judge of what weight their views should be given' (Archard, 2004, p.66).

Concluding comments

Educational inclusion has now been considered from the rights perspective. Children in particular (should) have their interests protected and advanced by multiple rights instruments and interconnected Articles. However, in reality, duty bearers ultimately control the extent to which children can exercise their rights. The guiding principles discussed above transcend from education into how we involve autistic children in research, including guidance from adults, voices being given due weight and being safe. In Chapter Five I discuss how researchers can develop rights-based participatory research and, in particular, highlight how we can help support participants in forming their views. First, in Chapter Four, I detail the efficacy of mainstream inclusion for autistic children, which for many demonstrates that their mainstream experiences are not that of inclusion or those promised by the rights instruments discussed above.

4 The efficacy of mainstream inclusion for autistic young people

Introduction

Increasingly, autistic children are being educated in mainstream schools, particularly if they are more academically able. This chapter presents a detailed synthesis of extant literature regarding the efficacy of mainstream inclusion for autistic children. I discuss literature exploring the perspectives of parents, teachers and, to a lesser extent, children and young people. I end the chapter by exploring the lived reality of bullying and mental health difficulties experienced by many within the autism community.

Context

Almost two decades ago the Department of Education for Northern Ireland (2002) reported that 39% of autistic children attended mainstream school in one education area in NI. Based on figures obtained from DENI's statistics branch (November 2018), in the year 2017/2018 the majority of 9,194 autistic pupils in NI, some 7,127 (77.5%), were educated in mainstream schools, a considerable increase. This is coupled with a decrease in the proportion of autistic children having a Statement of SEN, dropping from 74% in 2008/2009 to 58% in 2018/19 (Department of Health, Social Services and Public Safety, 2019). It is therefore reasonable to suggest that all mainstream teachers should expect to teach autistic children.

The debate

There is concern amongst parents, educators and autistic children themselves about the effectiveness of mainstream inclusion for all autistic children. There is a growing body of research which demonstrates a disconnect between the mainstream school environment, practice and the needs of autistic children; much of which is outlined in the remainder of this chapter. There is a misconception that, because many autistic children have academic ability (or are deemed 'high functioning'), they are automatically capable of coping in a mainstream school environment without adjustment or support. However, by having academic strengths they should not be considered as having a 'mild' form of autism; their difficulties are lived on a daily basis. This reiterates the need for sensitive and person-centred terminology to ensure autism and individual people are considered more broadly than 'function limited' terms.

Difficulties with mainstream inclusion arise from the interaction between the autistic child's intrinsic characteristics and factors within the school environment, including teacher understanding, teacher knowledge and sensory, social and geographical aspects of the school environment (Eldar, Talmor and Wolf-Zukerman, 2010; Keane et al., 2012). However, just to re-emphasise, recognising a child's individual challenges is not to say that the child is at fault, but, rather, highlights that there is often a mismatch between the mainstream school and their characteristics. For instance, the unpredictable social and sensory aspects of the environment can be overwhelming and the school environment can be antithetical to meeting their needs (Goodall, 2018c; McGregor and Campbell, 2001; Sproston, Sedgewick and Crane, 2017; Wing, 2007), although when the environment is supportive the child is more likely to flourish.

Wing (2007) discusses how some autistic children sit quietly while school staff assume they are coping and doing well – which is more typical of, but not limited to, autistic girls. Some do well, but others have developed a veneer of coping in school – camouflaging or perhaps withdrawing – and, when they return home, express their anxiety that has built up from trying to keep up with academic and social demands of the day. These young people may be progressing to some degree academically, but at the cost of 'inner turmoil'. Teachers should avoid saying to parents/carers, 'but s/he was fine all day in school …'

Autism-specific provision

Autistic children often benefit from having their own space within a highly organised and predictable classroom staffed with experienced, knowledgeable and skilled teachers. Wing (2007, p.28) suggests

> it is reasonable to ask why one should put a vulnerable child through the ordeal of mainstream schooling, making their anxiety

and social isolation much worse, because of the theories of idealists who have no knowledge or empathy for children with autism.

Although this statement may be considered tendentious, and non-representative of every child's experience, it is the reality for too many autistic children – including those discussed in this book. Autistic children may, therefore, benefit from the greater empathy, understanding and individual teaching input that smaller specialist schools, such as autism-specific schools, can provide (but which are non-existent in NI), or the positive educational experiences had by the autistic young people in alternative education, whom we hear from later (see Goodall, 2019).

Autistic children either feel that they belong and are included, or feel that they are an outsider looking in. Autism-specific schools potentially allow for the realisation of inclusion principles of empowerment, acceptance and belonging by offering a deliberately autism-specific environment saturated with an ethos of understanding (Goodall, 2015a; Lynch and Irvine, 2009). Specialist autism-specific schools have high staff-pupil ratios, with teachers' in-depth expertise enabling them to create more appropriate learning environments and to work effectively on the challenges associated with including autistic children.

Within a parent survey (n=317) commissioned by the voluntary group Northern Ireland Schools for Autism and Related Conditions (NISARC) in 2015 (discussed in Goodall, 2015a), 40% (n=127) placed stand-alone ASD schools as first or second preference for assisting their children in accessing suitable education. However, according to Ravet (2011), autism-specific schools could be viewed as a means of absolving mainstream teachers of the responsibility for teaching and meeting the needs of the autistic child, offering a get-out clause and, arguably, the mentality that only ASD experts can teach the child. I do appreciate Ravet's argument, but I am also mindful that it may be more beneficial for pupils to have the teachers in front of them who want to work with, understand and support them. Parsons et al. (2011, p.2) conclude from an international review of best practice that 'a range of educational provision should be maintained in order to cater appropriately for a wide diversity of need'.

Outcomes

Mainstream inclusion has been described as complex and poorly understood because of a lack of research that compares the outcomes of special education placements to mainstream (Smith, 2012). Educational research is also scarce when relating to outcomes for those transitioning from special schools to mainstream settings (Martin et al., 2019). Undoubtedly, mainstream inclusion can be enabling and beneficial – although examples were less readily reported within the literature. Benefits include displaying more social behaviour and increased social skills (Reiter and Vitani, 2007), as well as having more advanced education goals and develop coping strategies for times of transition and change (Eldar, Talmor and Wolf-Zukerman, 2010; Lindsay et al., 2013).

However, the mismatch between mainstream and many autistic children may result in challenging behaviour – or, perhaps more accurately described, anxiety-induced stressed behaviour in reaction to a challenging school environment with inflexible pedagogy and rigid mindsets. Challenging behaviour, outbursts of aggression and anxiety are thought of as linked due to neurobiological predisposition and the interplay with environmental stressors (Mazefsky et al., 2013). Anxiety experienced by autistic children is more likely to be externalised through acting-out behaviours, such as aggression, compared to non-autistic children (White et al., 2009). For me, this response to stress, due to the stressors outweighing the young person's coping strategies, results in stressed behaviour (again emphasising the importance of individual strategies, as noted in Chapter Two).

When discussing the effects and build-up of stress I like to use the analogy of a bucket filling with water – I use a real bucket to demonstrate this with pupils. The water represents stressors building up and, without holes being punched in the bucket, water will overflow. Holes represent the strategies the young person has in their toolbox: for example, breathing exercises (breathe in for seven seconds and out for 11, practising using a candle/bubbles and a scented object); muscle tension exercises; help scripts; and emotion thermometers and visual indicators, such as two different coloured small bricks, reversible wristbands or coloured cards (green indicating 'okay' and red indicating needing help or a need to exit the classroom). These can be used for all in the class. It is important to remember that autistic children often arrive at school with their buckets already close to overflowing, and often something seen by others as trivial can be the final drop of water, or stress, to cause the overflow (the meltdown or shutdown). Often to re-calibrate, especially if overloaded by sensory input, the adage of 'output blocks input' is useful, in that simple strategies such as listening to music can block the input of chattering, background noise or even the person's own breathing. The strategies noted are in addition to the environmental, attitudinal, pedagogical and curricular adjustments already in place within the school (see the pizza analogy I outlined earlier).

Mainstream exclusion

Restricting understanding of behaviour to 'challenging', 'defiant' or 'oppositional' perhaps underscores reports of a disproportionate number of mainstream school exclusions for children with SEN and/or autism. In particular, challenging behaviour associated with autistic children who have average or above intelligence can be misunderstood. Blame may be levelled solely at the child and not the environment within which they are educated, or by the teacher lacking understanding of what underpins the behaviour – again, emphasising the danger associated with terms such as 'high functioning'. For instance, I have heard phrases such as 'he is intelligent, he should know better', or 'surely he understands how his behaviour is affecting others' or 'he's bright and yet this is how he behaves'.

Children with SEN account for up to 70% of permanent exclusions in England (Department of Education, 2015). This is reflected in Timpson (2019), who also indicates that boys with SEN are at greater risk of exclusion. Figures requested from the Department of Education for NI unveil an interesting picture; first, the overall figures for suspensions across the periods 2013–2018 could not be disaggregated based on group (for example, ASD, ADHD and so on); positively, however, they show an overall decrease from 43.5% to 37.9% despite the percentage of pupils identified as having SEN increasing from 22.2% to 23.9%. However, mirroring England, the data for NI demonstrate that suspension rates for pupils with SEN are disproportionate in comparison to the school population across the years 2013–2018 (see Table 4.1). And unsurprisingly, as will be discussed later, the vast majority of suspensions occurred in post-primary education (approximately 85% across 2013–2018).

The Department for Education (2018) in England notes the substantial and increasing body of literature concerning autism and school exclusion. Alarmingly, educational exclusion rates for autistic pupils

Table 4.1 School suspension data

Year	Percentage of all pupils suspended	Percentage of pupils with SEN suspended
2013/14	1.32%	2.31%
2014/15	1.30%	2.12%
2015/16	1.47%	2.10%
2016/17	1.41%	2.03%
2017/18	1.41%	2.01%

Source: DENI March 2019

are more than twice the average for all pupils within England's state-funded schools (Department of Education, 2017), despite it being unlawful to exclude children due to their needs (Department for Education, 2012). As I noted in Goodall (2019, p.7), 'informal exclusion through isolation' is also widely reported in the media, with the recent Timpson Review of School Exclusion (Timpson, 2019) investigating these issues.

It is important to remember that exclusion from school not only impacts on educational experiences but can adversely influence future opportunities. The ongoing cost of exclusion in inclusion (or unsuccessful mainstream inclusion) extends beyond the person and impacts on society in terms of lost potential. Jordan (2008) suggests that we cannot persist with a system that is not meeting the needs of (all) autistic children or achieving the goals of an inclusive society, as discussed earlier. However, with continued persistence on narrow mainstream wedded inclusion we will persist with a system that cannot meet the needs of all. The importance of developing an education system that supports autistic young people to ensure they have a smoother transition to adulthood – as autistic adults – is summarised by Levy and Perry (2011, p.1275):

> the major factors affecting social outcomes in adulthood is the adequacy of educational provisions and access to appropriate education for later employment and social and economic independence.

Next, I will discuss literature that reports the perspectives of parents, teachers and autistic children on what enables inclusion, factors which act as barriers to inclusion and the suitability of mainstream inclusion. Other data and reports are threaded throughout the next sections, mainly regarding NI but applicable elsewhere.

Parental perspectives

The Northern Ireland Commissioner for Children and Young People (2007, p.13) reports that parents (n=59) identified enabling factors for mainstream education as training for staff, dedicated classroom assistance, good pastoral support and working in partnership with parents and the child. Conversely, barriers to a positive school experience were identified by parents as including lack of understanding from staff and pupils and unwillingness from staff to accommodate the specific needs of the child.

As children grow older, friendships perhaps become more selective and social relationships become more challenging within a more complex school environment (see Wainscot et al., 2008). The secondary school environment, from physical, geographical, social, emotional and academic aspects, is more unpredictable than in primary school and proves more challenging to the autistic young person. Children have to navigate busy corridors, move regularly between subjects while managing the organisation of books, lockers, different classroom layouts and seating arrangements, as well as building and maintaining relationships with, and understanding different expectations of, multiple teachers and a larger peer group. The social world in the teenage years is not only complex, but this is when young people develop their sense of identity and increasingly realise that they are different. And, as Brede et al. (2017, p. 2) summarise:

> It is well known that the social milieu becomes progressively more complex as children make their way through school, and this may be exacerbated by the mounting demands placed on students' academic progress.

These factors perhaps help explain why dissatisfaction levels are greater when children reach secondary school (Kasari et al., 1999) and why parental satisfaction is higher when the mainstream school has an ASD-specific resource base or unit (Frederickson, Jones and Lang, 2010). Units attached to schools for many pupils with SEN, including ASD, are more often conducive to learning than mainstream environments (Taylor, 2005). After a three-year period, teachers in ASD provisions embedded within schools reported that autistic children developed a range of skills, including improved behaviour that aided further targeted inclusion in mainstream classes (Bond and Hebron, 2015). Provisions such as these, and 'traditional' units attached to mainstream schools, allow children to settle in one smaller space and remove the need to navigate large areas of the school with greater number of peers, and, as Frederickson, Jones and Lang (2010) note, are more likely to have staff with more ASD training – offering a more nurturing approach.

The 2015 NISARC-commissioned survey (reported in Goodall, 2015a) found that 51% of the 317 parents ranked ASD units within mainstream schools as first or second preference for assisting their children in accessing suitable education, with some noting higher levels of training and the use of flexible strategies to better meet individual needs. Parents in Kidd and Kaczmarek (2010) noted that flexibility allowed their child to enjoy solitude, be alone and have time between academic activities to reduce stress levels and the risk of meltdown. These benefits were also noted by several parents in the NISARC survey who reported that there needs to be a 'quiet room for meltdown' in schools. Autistic children and young people rarely have opportunities to break away and relax from the ongoing social and sensory demands of the mainstream school environment (Attwood, 2007).

Parents also express concern about bullying in mainstream schools (a more detailed focus on bullying is presented later in this chapter). Increased incidences of bullying for autistic children help to explain parental dissatisfaction with mainstream schooling (O'Hagan and Hebron, 2017). Despite the concerns with bullying, Tobin et al. (2012, p.80) found that parents in their small-scale focus group study (n=7) wanted their children to attend mainstream in order to fit in and be part of the real world. Similarly, the National Autistic Society Northern Ireland (2012) reports that parents want their child's education to give them similar opportunities to other children, to be supportive of their child's needs and to be ambitious in their belief that their child can achieve. The society also reports that only half of parents believe their child is making good educational progress, with a third suggesting that the education their child receives is inadequate for meeting their needs. This can result in lower attendance at school. The NISARC survey reveals that, over a period of 60 school days, 9% of children missed between six and ten school days and a further 5% missed 20 days or more due to difficulties with interacting with the social and sensory environment (16 children missed 20 or more days out of 60). The experiences of the autistic young people presented later illustrate, in detail, why this is so.

Statistics provided by DENI (March 2019) in Table 4.2 show that mainstream school attendance figures for autistic children in primary and secondary are mostly lower than those who are not autistic. There is greater disparately when in post-primary education.

Overall, these differences appear relatively small, but the figures do not include those in home education (a statistic not held by DENI) – considered a growing option chosen by parents (see BBC, 2018). Studies suggest that some parents choose to home school their children as a result of non-enabling practices, in part to allow greater flexibility for when, what and how they learn (see Hurlbutt-Eastman, 2017).

Neither do the figures above include children who are on a part-time provision. For instance, the agreed provision may be such that the child is only required to attend part of the school day or week, yet this can allow for full attendance to be recorded, potentially skewing the attendance figures presented above. A hypothetical instance of this would be when a child is on a reduced timetabled provision of three days per week, and if they attend each of these three days they will

Table 4.2 Mainstream attendance figures

	2014/15	2015/16	2016/17	2017/18
Primary school				
Pupil enrolment with DYSLEXIA	94.6%	94.8%	94.6%	93.8%
Pupil enrolment with SEBD	93.6%	93.5%	93.5%	92.6%
Pupil enrolment with ASD	94.2%	94.2%	93.9%	94.9%
Pupil enrolment with ADHD	94.2%	94.2%	93.9%	93.0%
NI average	95.4%	95.5%	95.5%	94.9%
Post-primary school				
Pupil enrolment with DYSLEXIA	91.8%	91.9%	91.7%	91.8%
Pupil enrolment with SEBD	87.2%	87.4%	86.8%	87.4%
Pupil enrolment with ASD	92.9%	92.7%	92.0%	92.1%
Pupil enrolment with ADHD	90.6%	89.9%	89.8%	90.3%
NI average	93.4%	93.5%	93.3%	93.3%

Source: DENI statistics request, March 2019

accrue 100% attendance, as recorded, but in real terms they have only attended 60% of the school week. Nonetheless, the figures do indicate autistic children are absent from school more than the general school population. But compared to pupils with ADHD, SEBD or dyslexia, autistic pupils have what appears to be higher attendance in post-primary school – albeit these figures in isolation do not allow general conclusions to be made due to the aforementioned means by which attendance can be recorded. Note, however, that attendance rates *per se* are used as a measure of outcome and effectiveness during school inspection processes, so it is important to be mindful of what level of timetabled provision lies beneath each figure and perhaps by reducing a child's in-school provision the overall school attendance figure can be adjusted upwards.

Without adequate support, mainstream education can prove over-whelming, impacting on a young person's mental health – as attested by those we hear from later. For instance, 44% of parents in the NISARC survey (see Goodall, 2015a) report their child had consulted a doctor regarding anxiety, with 46% of parents stating that their child had been referred to mental health services and that 11% were taking medication as a result. According to parent respondents, anxiety and mental health issues have had such a deleterious effect on almost one in three of the children that they have talked about suicide or engaged in self-harming behaviour (see Goodall, 2015c). A small-scale study of ten parents of autistic children on social media revealed that their children's experiences of mainstream school were overwhelmingly negative (Goodall, 2015a; 2015c). One parent reported that her son 'punched himself in the face for two years because he could not cope with the noise and smells' (Goodall, 2015c, p.16). They describe how a lack of understanding by staff, mirrored in the NICCY study discussed earlier (Northern Ireland Commissioner for Children and Young People, 2007), resulted in her child being punished for displaying behaviours resulting from sensory overload. Another described how sensory overload resulted in her son becoming distressed the night before school. As a result, their child self-harms by 'smashing his face into the side of bunk beds until his nose bleeds, punching walls until his knuckles bleed. His mental health regularly takes a nose dive' (Goodall, 2015c, p.16).

Although these are the experiences of a small number of parents, they do support my contention, and that of others cited, that mainstream schools may not be able to meet the diverse and distinct needs of every autistic child. In my opinion, insistence on mainstream education may be doing more harm than good and perhaps these negative experiences, in part, explain why academic outcomes for autistic children are below their intellectual functioning. Requests to DENI's statistics branch (May, 2019) for the percentages of mainstream school leavers obtaining five GCSE A*-C grades (or equivalent), including English and Maths, exemplifies this for those with ASD, ADHD, 'social, emotional and behavioural difficulties' (SEBD) and dyslexia (Table 4.3), albeit against a positive uplift in GCSE attainment across the years 2015–2018. These figures are presented to highlight the achievement gap between autistic and non-autistic school leavers and also position autistic school leaver attainment alongside other categories of additional need. If GCSE English and Maths are removed, the attainment gap between all school

Table 4.3 Mainstream school leavers achieving five GCSE A*–C (or equivalent), including English and Maths

	2015/16	*2016/17*	*2017/18*
General school population	67.7%	69.6%	70.6%
ASD	50.0%	49.6%	53.0%
Dyslexia	37.7%	42.8%	43.4%
ADHD	27.9%	28.1%	36.1%
SEBD	17.4%	22%	36.1%

Source: DENI May 2019

leavers and those within the above groups narrows, demonstrating perhaps the difficulty with accessing English and Maths GCSE A*-C (for instance, in 2017/18 74.5% of autistic school leavers obtained 5 GCSE A*-C including equivalents, compared to 85.2% of all school leavers). The statistics also give insight into the potential cumulative impact for young people with co-occurring diagnoses, such as some of the young people in Chapters Six to Eight.

Such figures are in stark contrast to the much higher percentage of mainstream school leavers in general, despite school attendance figures highlighting a much narrower gap between those who are autistic and those who are not – hopefully this book addresses this conundrum of why. As the House of Commons Education and Skills Committee (2006, p.18) stated more than a decade ago, and this is still pertinent today, 'children with ASD provide an excellent example of where significant cracks exist in the system, to the detriment of those who fall between them'.

Teacher perspectives

Teacher training

As purported by parents, a lack of training is discussed by teachers as a barrier to inclusion (Cleary and Hayes, 2012; Humphrey and Symes, 2013). Effective provision (in part) emanates from knowledge of the individual autistic child and of the condition, but, as previously discussed, teachers must be mindful that autistic children may share the same diagnostic label but should not be considered as part of a homogeneous group. Myriad strategies and approaches are required to help support them, particularly as there has not been a singular approach suitable to all autistic learners (Parsons et al., 2011). Hayes et al. (2013) report that, despite mainstream school teachers believing they have adequate skills to support autistic children, they lack knowledge of crucial strategies and methodologies. This suggests a need for continuous ASD-specific professional development to support autistic children more effectively (Kucharczyk et al., 2015; Ravet, 2011).

Furthermore, training may not only aid inclusion but could be fundamental in the reduction of teacher 'burnout'. Understandably, and as will be discussed later in this book when considering educational improvement, large class sizes and a results-driven system place pressure upon teachers, and teacher burnout is common (Boujut et al., 2017). Teachers may also lack confidence for supporting autistic students (Gibb et al., 2007). They report that they want and need more autism-specific training (74% of teachers, n=65) (Goodall, 2010; 2012). A similar number (69%) felt their knowledge was not proficient to meet the needs of autistic children.

Teacher attitudes and experience

Successful implementation of inclusion relies heavily on the positive attitudes and willingness of teachers to support autistic young people (Lee et al., 2015; McGregor and Campbell, 2001; see also Segall and Campbell, 2012). In one such study by Humphrey and Symes (2013), teachers (n=53) viewed inclusion as both beneficial for supporting social inclusion but also as challenging for autistic young people, who have to develop strategies to cope within the mainstream environment. Young people in the latter parts of this book emphasise the importance of a supportive attitude, more so than the training a teacher has (see Chapters Five to Seven).

I also found that 60% of teachers (n=65) agreed with the inclusion of autistic children in mainstream schools, with several noting the need for these children to experience what it will be like in the real world (Goodall, 2010; 2012); an experience reflected by parents in Tobin et al. (2012) mentioned above. One teacher commented that 'each pupil with ASD has different needs and the attitudes of individual teachers also vary'. Those who did not agree with inclusion (only 12%) noted the pressures on teachers to meet academic standards (an issue highlighted in Chapter One). One teacher stated that teachers are already dealing with too many 'isms' (Goodall, 2010; 2012) – not an attitude that is conducive to supporting difference and striving for inclusion for all.

Aside from this pressure, negative attitudes from teachers towards autistic children may develop due to lack of understanding (Park, Chitiyo and Choi, 2010). Emam and Farrell (2009) found that the characteristics displayed by autistic children have a direct association with teachers' frustration, arguably transforming into teachers holding negative attitudes towards autistic children in future. Negative attitudes may, as a consequence, manifest in negative relationships between the teacher and autistic child which could contribute to the child being less socially accepted by peers. This, then, could result in negative peer awareness – a ripple effect.

Peer awareness is also instrumental for implementing inclusion for autistic children, as indicated by 17 teachers (n=21) in a qualitative study by Majoko (2016). And, to extend peer awareness to peer support, Coleman-Fountain (2017) emphasises the significance of an autistic child finding support in, and the formation of a positive sense of self from, connections with others who embrace an autistic identity. The young people we hear from across Chapters Five to Seven indicate the sense of camaraderie in sharing similar difficulties of educational experiences as others in aiding their feeling of belonging and inclusion (see also Goodall, 2019).

Wing (2007) suggests that educators should be guided by the daily experiences of autistic children and not their ideological position (see Chapter Five). This was reflected by teachers (n=8) in a study by McGillicuddy and O'Donnell (2014); hands-on experience, rather than training, enabled them to teach autistic children. Undoubtedly experiences impact on beliefs, future expectations and social representation of autistic children and their inclusion in mainstream schools (Linton et al., 2015). Attitudes towards inclusion are complex and impact teacher confidence in providing inclusive pedagogy (Arthur-Kelly et al., 2013) – experience alone will not guarantee successful inclusion or foster positive expectations. In line with the findings of studies explored above, I identified key factors which can help promote inclusive practice in the classroom, including: effective use of training; positive attitudes from teachers, parents and peers; and knowledge of the condition and strategies. However, barriers to effective inclusion from teacher perspectives include: large class sizes; negative attitudes from teachers; lack of knowledge or training; and intolerance from peers (Goodall, 2010; 2012). To enable effective inclusion, Morewood, Humphrey and Symes (2011) advocate a saturation model underpinned by staff training, peer awareness education, school environment modification, flexible provision and a positive ethos of autism acceptance, celebrating difference and suitable policy.

Child perspectives

The existing research, albeit sparse, demonstrates that autistic children and young people themselves can find inclusion in mainstream schools stressful, marked by experiences of bullying, isolation and anxiety (Brede et al., 2017; Hebron and Humphrey, 2014; Humphrey and Lewis, 2008a, 2008b; Humphrey and Symes, 2011; Poon et al., 2014; Sproston, Sedgewick and Crane, 2017).

Despite these experiences, autistic children express the same desire to be included and develop peer friendships as non-autistics (O'Hagan and Hebron, 2017). Gibb et al. (2007) contend that both social and academic inclusion are important aspects of a child's educational experience. However, Saggers, Hwang and Mercer (2011), who interviewed nine students with ASD, and Sciutto et al. (2012), who carried out an online survey with 27 adults with Asperger's retrospectively commenting on education, discuss mixed attitudes of students with autism to socialising with peers: some preferred time alone, some liked engaging in conversations centred on their interests, while others found the social (and academic) aspect of school stressful. Moyse and Porter (2015) carried out observations on three autistic girls (aged 7–11) attending mainstream primary schools and followed these up with interviews with them (and their teachers and mothers). The girls spoke of the difficulties they had working collaboratively with others and with interacting with peers, particularly in the playground and at unstructured times – they indicated that this was mainly due to not being included by peers. Other studies focusing on autistic girls, such as Sproston, Sedgewick and Crane (2017) which involved eight girls, found they experienced inappropriate sensory environments, a lack of staff understanding of their needs and how to support them, and inflexible approaches to their inclusion in class or elsewhere.

Mirroring teacher perspectives, Ambler, Eidels and Gregory (2015) used two psychometric assessments and found that autistic high school students (n=52) in Australia self-reported more symptoms of anxiety and feelings of anger than non-autistic peers (n=52). Further, and as suggested earlier, stressors accumulate throughout the day and can result in the antecedent to an incident of challenging behaviour being seen as trivial and disproportional (Ambler, Eidels and Gregory, 2015). Anxiety can stem from the need for predictability and routine and, as I indicated earlier, is reported as more common for autistic girls than boys (Solomon et al., 2012; Rose and Rudolph, 2006). Humphrey and Lewis (2008a, p.38) explored the experiences of autistic young people and conclude that the 'chaos of the corridor' experienced in mainstream schools opposes this need for predictability and routine.

Humphrey and Lewis (2008b) offered 20 11–17-year-old students with AS or 'high-functioning' autism multiple means of representation to share their experiences of mainstream education. Isolation, bullying and feelings of difference were noted. The children stated that safe havens, friendships and understanding teachers supported their inclusion (see also Parsons et al., 2011 and Safran, 2002). Bullying was also seen as a major concern for the four students with Asperger's interviewed by Hebron and Humphrey (2014), mirroring findings in other studies (see Humphrey and Symes, 2010; O'Hagan and Hebron, 2017). The Northern Ireland Commissioner for Children and Young People (2007) explored the views of 35 children and found that while 50% were quite or very satisfied with their school experience, 57% wanted teachers to have greater understanding of AS and provide better support. Further, 66% would like their school experience to be significantly different, particularly with respect to bullying and the need for safe learning environments.

Understanding was important for two adults with Asperger's in a study of school experience by Sciutto et al. (2012); they spoke of how their behaviour in school was misunderstood and that a lack of autism knowledge underpinned this. Students with autism viewed teacher flexibility as an enabler of inclusive practices and wanted support to be unobtrusive to avoid differences being highlighted (Saggers, Hwang and Mercer, 2011; Sciutto et al., 2012). Scuitto et al. (2012) identified two aspects of support that had a positive impact on the educational experiences of the adults with Asperger's who took part in their study; incorporating the child's interest into the curriculum and offering choice and responsibility rather than forcing them to conform. There is growing emphasis on the importance of tapping into and utilising a child's interests.

Recently Wood (2019) emphasised the importance of facilitating children's interests in the classroom. This not only benefits them in accessing the curriculum and learning, but can reduce school-based anxiety. Milton (2017, p.1674) also contends that when an autistic child's interests, attention and motivation are attended to, benefits may ensue for them and adults working with them. Benefits include improved social and communication abilities and positive impacts on emotional well-being and moderation of arousal or regulation (Winter-Messiers, 2007). And, as Gunn and Delafield-Butt (2016, p.411) write, using intense interests enables autistic children 'to relax, overcome anxiety, reduce stress, experience pleasure and make better sense of the physical world' and helps 'bring the child into the classroom' (p.425). This can bring us, as educators and researchers, into their world and bolster connections and rapport, the value of which cannot be underestimated.

A study of adolescents (seven autistic and 13 not) revealed that, despite being involved in the social structure of their classroom, the autistic children experienced more loneliness than their non-autistic peers (Locke et al., 2010). Moyse and Porter (2015, p.198) suggest that 'masking behaviours' influence the 'perception that others had of the impact of autism on their lives in school'. Autistic girls are at particular emotional and social risk because of the isolation experienced by being off the social radar and having to continually observe and judge the nuances of social situations (Rose and Rudolph, 2006). As suggested, females expend more cognitive effort on camouflaging and report greater anxiety than males (Lai et al., 2017; Livingston et al., 2019). Interestingly, however, Chamberlain, Kasari and Rotheram-Fuller (2007) studied the social networks in classrooms with an autistic child and uncovered a complex picture. Using self-report measures, autistic children do not perceive themselves to be lonely, yet their peers rated them as less socially accepted than non-autistic peers, albeit not equating to loneliness. Three adolescents in a study of friendship by O'Hagan and Hebron (2017) expressed a desire for friendship, yet experienced loneliness. What this demonstrates is that we ought to separate the difficulties autistic children may have with social interaction from the (misconceived) notion that they lack interest in developing friendship.

This small but significant body of research, from the perspectives of autistic children and young people, in addition to those from parents and teachers, demonstrates that mainstream inclusion – as it stands – is inappropriate for every autistic child. Moreover, the findings of Parsons (2015), who surveyed 55 autistic adults, suggest that the experiences of school do really matter; those who expressed positivity about school felt more positive about current life circumstances.

A focus on bullying and autism

As noted, bullying is a concern for autistic young people and those who are positioned to support them (including parents and teachers). It is widely reported that bullying disproportionately affects autistic children and young people (for instance, Humphrey and Hebron, 2015). Humphrey and Symes (2012) suggest that autistic children are three times more likely to be bullied than non-autistic peers. These figures may underplay the issue, as some may not readily identify that they are being bullied and unwittingly mistake a peer's attempt to tease or humiliate as 'friendly' (National Autistic Society, 2006).

It is suggested that bullying of autistic children in mainstream schools is widespread as a consequence of them being viewed as different (Monteith et al., 2002). Autistic people can find subtle nuances of social interaction and communication ambiguous; for example, body language, intonation of voice and the plethora of unwritten social rules. Therefore, autistic children may appear dissimilar, finding it difficult to relate to non-autistic peers. And, conversely, non-autistic peers may fail to understand or relate to autistic young people, signifying the importance of reciprocal, or joint, empathy and of peer awareness in schools.

Eslea et al. (2004) indicate greater susceptibility of bullying for children who are isolated and play alone. However, from experience in the AEP it is evident that those autistic young people who prefer to enjoy their own company, rather than trying to interact, are less likely to experience bullying. This is perhaps because their aloofness seems esoteric to individuals who may perpetrate bullying. Conversely, some who regularly attempt to socialise and integrate, perhaps in a manner which is not in keeping with their peer group, are the ones who experience bullying, or, at the very least, teasing and ostracising. Unfortunately these children may become wearisome of initiating and developing peer relationships based on previous negative experiences of social rejection, resulting in further social isolation. Again, this becomes particularly pertinent during adolescence when life in the social world – of education and beyond – becomes increasingly complex.

A focus on mental health and autism

I feel it is important to increase awareness of the varied difficulties experienced by autistic people, such as increased susceptibility to mental health issues, which are also reflected by the young people later in this book (and experienced by many young people I teach). Hirvikoski et al. (2016) (reported in Autistica, 2016) write that autistic adults (without learning difficulties) are nine times more likely to die from suicide than the general population. Many studies identify a high incidence of mental health issues such as anxiety, depression and suicidal ideation in autistic people stemming from risk factors such as social isolation, social exclusion and unemployment (see Cassidy et al., 2014). Females in particular may expend considerable cognitive effort to camouflage or compensate for social difficulties to gain social capital, which can lead to poorer mental health, including increased stress, anxiety and depression (Cage and Troxell-Whitman, 2019; Lai et al., 2017; Livingston et al., 2019; see also Baldwin and Costley, 2016). And, with regard to autistic young people in general, the effort required to keep up the façade of 'normal' can be exhausting – they may not feel supported to be the person they are. Without understanding this exertion and making allowances or offering support – such as reduced homework, allotting more 'alone' or 'down' time in class – these young people can, and do, flounder. I remember a young autistic adult telling me of the 'social hangover' she experiences after intensely social events, such as family gatherings, and her need for a lot of time to rebuild mental and physical energy the following day.

Some young autistic adults in a study by Crane et al. (2018) felt that their mental health problems resulted from the pressure to act normal (or camouflaging) in a neurotypical world and that they were 'often seen as too "normal" to be autistic' (p.484). The mental health experiences of these young autistic adults (n=130, aged 16–25 years) in England suggest that we should listen to – and learn from – young people to ensure their mental health needs are being met. What the study identified, via an online survey (n=109) and detailed interviews (n=21), is that autistic young people have difficulty in evaluating their mental health, experience high levels of stigma and face obstacles when accessing support. Young autistic women appeared to have a particularly difficult time, underscored by delays in diagnosis. They highlighted that if non-autistic people had to grow up being excluded, bullied and pressured to be something they are not they would likely develop the same conditions. Having to negotiate reasonable adjustment time and time again to access support and gain understanding can add to the perception of self as pathologised (see Hodge, Rice and Reidy, 2019). This underscores the importance of pursuing and emphasising autism acceptance and personalisation, rather than normalisation, to help the young people build their sense of self.

Concluding comments

I have highlighted research, from the perspectives of parents, teachers and autistic young people themselves, which demonstrates mainstream inclusion is not suitable for all autistic young people. There remains a dearth in literature regarding the educational experiences of autistic young people and their thoughts on inclusion, particularly from their viewpoint.

Many calls exist for gathering their experiences and views on education to better inform policy and practice (Parsons, 2015). O'Neil (2008, p.787) suggests, and as this book champions, instead of ignoring or silencing autistic people 'it is time to lend them our ears. Who better to ask about what ASD really is than someone who lives with it every day?' Wing (2007, p.33) questions, as this book aims to answer, 'why do we not find from the children themselves what kind of schooling is best for them?' The lives and experiences of these children should be our guide to improving education, not ideology. The experiences of 12 autistic young people are included throughout the remainder of this book.

5 Researching with autistic young people

Introduction

The voices of autistic young people remain limited in research concerning their educational experiences, their thoughts on school improvement and of what inclusion means to them. This chapter, divided into two sections, provides a theoretical and practical framework to help support educators and researchers in involving these young people (and others) in authentic, participatory and rights-respecting research.

Section One introduces educational research. I focus on the use of qualitative research to gain greater understanding of the lived experiences of autistic young people. By reflecting on my own study, alongside research literature, I want to address potential 'dilemmas' associated with gathering and representing the voices of autistic young people and why these young people's voices remain limited within research. I end by exploring student voice and participation (including models of participation).

I then begin Section Two and here I explore participatory autism research. By adhering to several core principles we can remove attitudinal and practical barriers and thereby create inclusive research which supports autistic young people in forming, presenting and having their views heard. These principles include: ethical considerations (such as power imbalance and being a practitioner-researcher); communication considerations (including supporting a range of communication preferences); and using the expertise of a Children's Research Advisory Group (CRAG) to advise on the methods and data collection activities. I also outline the rationale for, and description of, the participatory methods I used. I end Section Two by outlining my approach to data analysis and discussing the concepts of trustworthiness and authenticity in qualitative research.

SECTION ONE

Educational research

Educational research is contested in terms of how it should be done, for what purposes and by whom. Research is traditionally carried out by academics, rather than classroom practitioners, arguably creating a vacuum between what is theory and what is useful for the teacher in the classroom. To reconcile this, and strengthen the relevance for classroom teachers, there is growing emphasis on teachers carrying out research as practitioner-researchers. Later, I revisit the advantages of 'wearing two hats' in my role as a practitioner-researcher in developing authentic and inclusive participatory research methods; namely the experience of building relationships with, gaining understanding of, and designing educational programmes for, many autistic young people during my career.

Educational research, irrespective of whether it is qualitative, quantitative or of mixed methods, should strive to capture the complexities of education and learning. It hopefully enlightens us, informs our understanding and, perhaps, challenges – or at least questions – perceptions on a particular issue (such as the impact of mainstream 'inclusion' for all, or the merits of autistic voice research). Primarily, for me, it should develop an understanding of 'why', and then, as a result, should influence educational policy and shape pedagogy – the 'how' – to better support pupils, particularly those who are at risk of educational exclusion, such as autistic children. With regard to the education of autistic young people, we should engage with them directly and seek out their lived experiences, their feelings, their narratives and, importantly, their ideas and advice on how we can better support them. In simple terms, by doing this we will enhance our understanding of what works and what does not.

Why I followed a qualitative path

Policymakers appear to prefer quantitative research outputs, perhaps due to the definiteness in supporting an argument or, indeed, the ability to offer generalisations or draw conclusions to a certain level of probability (Davies, 2007). Basically, quantitative research produces numerical data for analysis and does not give meaning or in-depth insights into social constructs or phenomena. As education is more nuanced and complex than a scaled response in a survey can hope to uncover, I developed a qualitative-based approach to explore and understand the voices and educational experiences of autistic young people. As will be seen when I detail my approaches in more detail in Section Two, I used numerical data and tools (such as scoring schools out of ten) within my interview schedules as concrete (non-abstract) points of reference from which to develop discussion further.

However, I avoided a quantitative approach as it would not allow me to explore in-depth experiences and because I know the young people I work with do not respond well to quantitative survey-based methods of research. I have watched as many got bored partway through a questionnaire and tick items quickly with little care, understanding or attention in order to get 'the work' finished.

Qualitative research demands a large skill set – from developing appropriate methods, building trusting and ongoing relationships with participants, being immersed in the context of data collection and then recording, organising and analysing large amounts of textual data. Fundamentally for me, and as stated by Conn (2015, p.65), 'qualitative research methods are often pinned on the making of a good social connection with the child'.

Qualitative research can elicit the unquantifiable knowledge of individual experiences and interpretations, while verbatim quotes often reveal the saliency of data. Denzin and Lincoln (2011) describe qualitative research as identifying meaning, perspectives and understanding, relying more on words, feelings and narratives than on numerical data. Qualitative research is not concerned with large sample sizes, generalisation, replication or with hypothesis testing *per se*. In qualitative research, the quantitative concepts of validity and reliability are replaced with the terms 'trustworthiness' and 'authenticity' to establish confidence in the findings (Guba, 1981; Lincoln and Guba, 1985). I outline a framework I used to enhance 'trustworthiness' and 'authenticity' in Section Two.

Autistic children in research

The motto 'nothing about us without us' foregrounds the need for disabled people to be involved in all aspects of decision-making about disability, including research. As Cohen, Manion and Morrison (2011, p.219) espouse, 'the social and educational world is a messy place … it has to be studied in total rather than in fragments if a true understanding is to be reached'. By remaining narrowly focused on adult perspectives – without the voices and input from children and young people directly – our understanding will remain fragmented, the most important voices will remain unheard and our picture of autism and mainstream education, and of inclusion for autistic learners, will remain incomplete. To re-emphasise, the views of autistic young people ought to be sought; they are invaluable for enhancing our understanding of what education is like for them, and how as educational practitioners, policy-makers, researchers and academics we can empower and improve the lives of more children.

The perspectives of autistic children remain limited, particularly within qualitative research and even more so with regard to rights-informed participatory research. There is a recurrent 'call to arms' for more 'voice' research with autistic young people (see Fayette and Bond, 2018). However, Humphrey and Parkinson (2006) suggest that autistic people can be marginalised within educational contexts, with research conducted on rather than with them. Further, Milton (2012) questions the reliability of a knowledge base created largely from the opinions of non-autistic stakeholders; he calls for more autistic young people to be involved in the pursuit of knowledge-construction about autistic people to help ensure there is relevance for them (see Milton, 2014).

Limited research may be a result of an unwillingness to involve autistic children because of (perceived) methodological challenges arising from associated difficulties with social communication (Ellis, 2017; Harrington et al., 2013; Preece and Jordan, 2010), inflexibility in thought (Wing, 1996), and their perceived vulnerability (Lewis, 2009). Some autistic children are believed to have difficulty in recalling and presenting personal experiences (Brown et al., 2012), identifying and expressing emotions (Preece and Jordan, 2010) and processing infor-mation (Attwood, 2007; Jordan, 2005), with concerns raised regarding the reliability of self-reporting (Pandolfi, Magyar and Dill, 2012). However, to deny them their voice, by positioning them as deficit and 'too difficult' to involve in research, not only denies them their rights but also restricts our understanding. And, as I present, with the correct approach many of these perceived difficulties can be overcome. Never-theless, Rose and Shevlin (2017, p.68) propose that, despite more edu-cational researchers striving to engage children and young people in research, and thus trying to show that their views are valued, it should not be assumed that this is an easy process. Autistic adults report sev-eral major deterrents to participation, namely practical issues such as travel, but, importantly to the discussion that follows, also perceived tokenism, insensitivity of researchers and, crucially, a limited choice of ways to participate (Haas et al., 2016).

More needs to be done to actively push the boundaries of participa-tion for autistic young people within research by identifying creative and flexible approaches to provide them with opportunities to express their views. For instance, if social interaction is a concern then adopting a one-to-one approach will better support each individual young person (discussed below). And, as General Comment No. 9 on the Rights of Children with Disabilities states, 'children should be provided with whatever mode of communication they need to facilitate expressing their views' (United Nations, 2006b, para.32). O'Neil (2008, p.791) states that 'communication is not synonymous with speech, or even face-to-face encounters. Many autistics excel in communication through other means'. Therefore, preferring (or needing) an alternative means of communicating was not considered to be an inability to express their views. The researcher is responsible for bridging the gap between communication preferences and how these are supported in practice. Accordingly, I used multiple adaptive and flexible approaches to help participants form and express their experiences that did not rely on a singular mode of communication. As I discuss in greater detail in Section Two, I remained flexible and at times took my lead from the young people. I used supporting visual cues, multiple modes of communication (such as oral, written and drawing) and scaffolding measures to support participants in having their voices heard, as necessitated by Article 12 of the UNCRC and Article 7 of the UNCRPD.

I now briefly highlight the benefits of student voice and listening to the young people's educational experiences before outlining models of participation which can be used, as I did, to gauge how participatory a research project is (or any other programme in school seeking the views of pupils).

Student voice

Cremin, Mason and Busher (2011, p.600) suggest that 'schools are increasingly expected, and even required, to engage with young people's voices'. However, there may be a reluctance to truly engage with pupil voice and it has been widely suggested that participation (and student voice) has become so mainstreamed in schools it is in danger of resulting in empty rhetoric (Cook-Sather, 2007). Concerns have also been raised more widely over research which celebrates giving voice to children (Hammersley, 2017), premised, in part, on restricted conceptions of how we access and allow children to present their voice, and adult influences in the weight afforded to the children's construction of their narratives. As a precautionary note, researchers can fall into the trap of using tokenistic 'participatory' approaches in order to meet an obligation to seek the views of children which serves no greater purpose than that (Mannion, 2007).

However, there are many benefits to participation. Children develop intra- and interpersonal capabilities, increase competency and build their confidence, agency and autonomy (Lansdown, 2011). They are listened to, validated and have their experiences affirmed. This creates a 'virtuous circle', whereby children become empowered and their status is enhanced as capable people with insightful perspectives who can effect change within schools. This can benefit the person, practice and legislation (see Lundy and Stalford, 2013).

Two models I now present helped guide my research; and, by using these, one can quickly judge whether or not their research can be described as participatory.

Models of participation

Hart's model (represented in Figure 5.1), adapted from Arnstein's (1969) 'eight rungs on the ladder of citizen participation', represents a series of hierarchical levels that can be used as a measuring stick for assessing the quality of participation within a programme or project, such as research. The first three rungs, categorised as non-participation levels, are manipulation, decoration and tokenism. An example of manipulation would be adults using children to hold placards against a divisive issue but without their having an understanding or involvement beyond the photograph that is used to 'bolster their cause' (Hart, 1992, p.9). Tokenism describes situations when children are described as having a voice but 'have little or no choice about the subject or the style of communicating it, and little or no opportunity to formulate their own opinions' (Hart, 1992, p.9). On rung four a project would be considered participatory; children are 'assigned but informed' and have a meaningful role. They volunteer for a project only after being informed about the purpose and intentions of the project (such as research). Projects or research can be judged as more participatory when children move from being consulted (rung five) to being co-researchers involved in making decisions (rung six) to children inviting adults to join them in decision-making (rung eight). This ladder analogy has been interpreted as sequential steps that build children's competence in participation (Hart, 2008).

An alternative participation model (Figure 5.2) is offered by Shier (first presented in 2001, later revisited in 2006, and found in Boylan and Dalrymple, 2009). This model does not offer any equivalent levels to Hart's lower three rungs. Shier (2001, p.110) acknowledges that these lower rungs are most beneficial in helping researchers and educators identify 'false types of participation'. Shier revised his original 2001 'Pathway to Participation' model – becoming 'Pathways to Participation' – to reflect the evolution of his thinking and to make visible

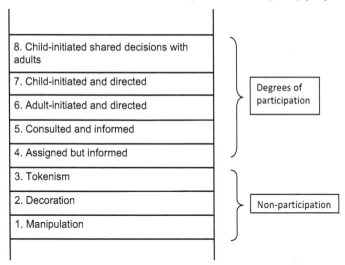

Figure 5.1 Representation of Hart's Ladder of Participation

multiple pathways, rather than a singular path to participation (2019, personal correspondence). The 'Pathways to Participation' model is based on 15 questions across five levels of participation and indicates the point at which the UNCRC is endorsed. The levels of participation are: (1) children are listened to; (2) children are supported in expressing their views; (3) children's views are taken into account; (4) children are involved in decision-making processes; and (5) children share power and responsibility for decision-making. The model presents the relationships between the various levels of participation and the stages within each. Shier (2006) cautions that different levels of participation are appropriate in different circumstances, therefore being at the top of each model is not always best.

I used Shier's (2001, p.116) original 'Pathway to Participation' model as a 'usable tool' to evaluate the participatory level of my study: the children and young people were listened to (level 1); they were supported in expressing their views (level 2); they had their views taken into account regarding their school experiences and during the Children's Research Advisory Group (CRAG) (level 3); and children were invited to join in the decision-making through this CRAG (level 4). My study surpassed the point needed to be considered as endorsing the UNCRC (as indicated in Figure 5.1), so is considered to endorse and also apply the principles of the UNCRC. It also adhered to a Children's Rights-Based Approach (CRBA).

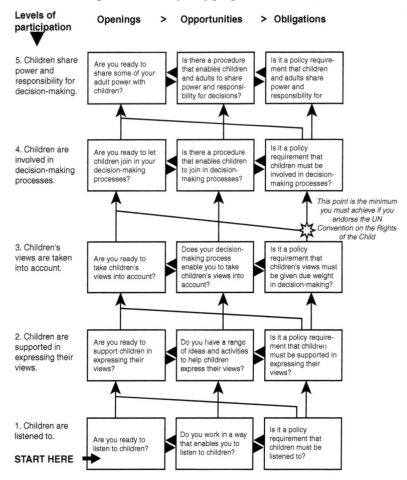

Figure 5.2 Pathways to Participation (Shier, 2001; and revisited 2006)
Source: found in Boylan and Dalrymple (2009)

Children's Rights-Based Approach (CRBA)

A Children's Rights-Based Approach is based on the application of the principles of a human rights-based approach (see Lundy and McEvoy, 2012; United Nations, 2003), and has implications for all stages of the research process: research aims should be informed by the CRC standards; the research process should comply with the CRC standards; and research outcomes should build the capacity of children, as rights-holders, to claim their rights and build the capacity

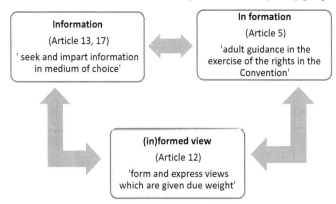

Figure 5.3 Assisting children to an informed view (adapted from Lundy and McEvoy, 2011, p.141)

of duty-bearers to fulfil their obligations. Cutting across all of this is a requirement to ensure that the process furthers the realisation of children's rights. This current study adheres to the CRBA employed in the Centre for Children's Rights at Queen's University, Belfast, where I completed my Doctorate. Particular emphasis was placed on children's participatory rights in which participants are assisted in both forming and expressing their views and experiences.

Lundy and McEvoy (2011) developed a methodological approach (Figure 5.3) that I also used to guide me in assisting children to informed views. The method demonstrates the interconnectedness of various UNCRC articles, such as the right to information (Articles 13 and 17) and guidance from adults (Article 5) while the child's view is in formation. This assists children in expressing what is then both a formed and an informed view (Article 12).

These connected rights underpin participatory autism research, as I now discuss in Section Two.

SECTION TWO

Participatory autism research

Scott-Barrett, Cebula and Florian (2018, p.17) state that:

> if we wish to make meaningful progress in the way we seek and listen to the views of young people with autism, then we need to

engage with the methodological and ethical complexities that can and do occur in research in this field.

By recognising and removing attitudinal and practical barriers to participation – through framing our questions, designing our methods and disseminating our findings in a way that is respectful and embracing of autistic differences – we can develop truly inclusive participatory and rights-based research. Doing so will enhance the entire research process for researcher and participant. Some core principles to follow, as I detail later, include, but are not limited to: involving children and young people in the research design (such as the use of a CRAG to ensure the development of applicable and meaningful methods); being mindful of, and finding out, the communication preferences of participants (and by proactively incorporating multiple modes of representation); and considering the sensory environment within the data collection setting (such as lighting, noise levels, room layout, not wearing clothes with distracting patterns or products with strong scents).

For meaningful and effective participation, attention must be applied to all four aspects of Lundy's (2007) widely cited model of participation (space, voice, audience and influence; see Figure 3.1 in Chapter Three). These aspects are specific obligations placed on duty bearers under Article 12 of the UNCRC. Children and young people should be:

- Provided with a safe and inclusive space to express their views, an aspect I discuss further below (space);
- Provided with appropriate information, guidance and means to express their views, again an aspect I detail further (voice);
- These views are communicated to someone with the responsibility to listen (audience);
- Views are taken seriously and acted upon when appropriate (influence).

Building rapport, being respectful, showing empathy through research design, understanding autism as diverse, and listening and learning in the process of co-construction of knowledge with participants in advance of – and throughout – the entire research process help to develop research that is participatory; as do addressing the potential for power imbalance and avoiding assumptions about young persons' capabilities by positively recognising them as experts in their lives (see Pellicano et al., 2017; Scott-Barrett, Cebula and Florian, 2018).

Researcher mindsets must also promote the attitude that autistic people have something of importance to offer. Milton, Mills and Pellicano (2014, p.2650) argue:

We believe that human dignity requires us to make every effort to access the views and perspectives of autistic people. The absence of any sustained attempt to represent the views of autistic individuals ... threatens further to disempower those already frequently overlooked in key decision-making processes that shape their lives.

Power imbalance

A key principle of participatory research is the recognition, and undermining, of the traditional power imbalance between researcher and participant. This has been discussed at length (see Aluwihare-Samaranayake 2015; Robinson and Taylor 2013). However, there may be greater disparity when a participant has SEND that causes them some difficulties with communication. The power differential that exists between practitioner-researcher and participant can be difficult to overcome. This, however, should be acknowledged and not forgotten and researchers should actively seek ways – as I now present – to address and redress this and not simply problematise power differentials.

As a practitioner-researcher I acknowledged the power status and potential influence that my being a teacher might have had on those in the Alternative Education Provision (AEP), where the school, as a social setting, is organised around the power of the adults. Being in this position, as both a teacher and researcher, could have influenced a young person's participation and their willingness to be open and discuss their experiences. For those participants outside the AEP I also recognised that my position as a teacher could have evoked negative feelings because of past experiences within education.

Winstone et al. (2014) note that autistic young people may be influenced by a perceived power imbalance into thinking there is one correct answer to a question posed by the researcher. When the researcher is still seen as being in the 'teacher' role there is also a risk of participants interpreting the activities as school work. To overcome this I emphasised that the participants were the experts and that there were no correct or incorrect responses. I positioned myself as a knowing adult, but also as a learner keen to learn from the young people's experiences. I repeatedly emphasised the importance of the young person's position as expert and that their voices and experiences were of value. Mannion (2007) also suggests that the interwoven relationship between children, adults and the space they inhabit needs consideration. The research space – as I now discuss – was one step in reducing power imbalance.

The research space

The research space contributes to the efficacy of the research process, especially with children and young people (Hill, 2006). There needs to be 'legitimate and valued spaces in which students can speak' (Cook-Sather, 2002, p.4; see Lundy, 2007). Different spaces embody certain norms, rules and expectations. For example, the inference of correctness and academic performance of a classroom could be overbearing, thus impacting on participation.

I provided the participants with an appropriate, comfortable, safe and familiar space. For participants attending the busy AEP a small room off the main corridor was used. This room is often used for one-to-one personal work and is viewed as an established safe, private, conversational, neutral – yet serious – environment. It is well lit by natural light, has comfortable seating and is positioned in a quiet area of the AEP. Similar consideration was given for participants outside the AEP.

The study hub they attend was ideal for providing a safe, familiar and non-threatening environment, in a place they felt a belonging with other young people. This helped participants feel comfortable and able to explore their educational experiences. I considered potential aspects of the sensory environment within the room (the room had lots of natural light so electric lighting was not used). This room was next to the main room used for their study group, meaning parents were close by if sessions became too overwhelming. I also re-arranged the room layout to best support the young people. There was a lot of open, uncluttered space if the young person wished to move around (or stim) or leave, with clearly zoned areas to help with transitioning between different activities. For instance, during the interview participants were asked to select feelings to describe mainstream school. I set up an area of seating in a horseshoe shape; each chair had an A4 sheet with a feeling and an accompanying emoticon, which the young person could move along to decide which best represented their feelings of mainstream school. The majority of data collection took place around one area. Two comfortable seats were placed, angled towards each other, at a table to add to the ethos of knowledge co-creation, thus helping to reduce power imbalances (much like they would in a counselling scenario). This helped create a more relaxed and less intense interaction than facing each other across a table. The young person was positioned close to the door, but not in direct view of anyone passing by, to allow them to exit easily if necessary.

Ethical considerations

Addressing power imbalance is one ethical consideration. I now briefly outline several others, all of which are applicable to developing inclusive participatory research (yet also help to redress the balance of power). I focus mainly on informed consent, more specifically the importance of ensuring participants have information provided in an accessible and meaningful way (see Scott-Barrett, Cebula and Florian, 2018). This is not only a matter of ethics, but rights, as discussed earlier (see Figure 5.2 for example).

Steps were taken to ensure that informed consent was obtained from each participant, which encompassed four elements: having understanding of the research; voluntary participation; explicit written consent; and renegotiable participation. The latter – the right to withdraw – was reiterated at the start of each data collection session. Participants were informed of their right to withdraw up to the point when the data was made anonymous, emphasising that consent was renegotiable. At every stage they were protected from harm (the right to protection) with methods designed that would contribute to participants' wellbeing.

The capacity to give informed consent relies on the quality of the information provided: this was given in various forms. An information sheet was provided to all participants and their parents/guardians. This sheet was shown to two young people in the AEP to check readability, and, through unambiguous language and a question and answer format, potential benefits of the research were highlighted; namely that it could make education better for them and other children. However, no promises were made that this would definitely result from taking part.

Once the young people in the AEP had expressed an interest in taking part in the research they were given the opportunity to openly ask questions about it. Similarly, those children outside the AEP were given my email address on the consent letter to further discuss the research before commencing, or throughout. I met parents of the young people from outside the AEP to ensure informed consent was obtained. I created a private social media page. Parents were invited and then a short video of me introducing myself and describing the research was uploaded for parents to show their children. This helped ensure these participants could have the information provided in a manner that would mean they were informed of the study and their role within it, and, second, to reassure them about me as the 'unknown' researcher prior to meeting with them. This page also allowed parents to detail any considerations for working with their children. In addition, an introductory session was held to get to know those participants outside the AEP a little better – and for them to get to know me prior to them giving their consent.

Prior to commencing data collection, participants chose a pseudonym which was applied to their data. This helped to ensure anonymity yet allowed each participant to identify their data. Participants were also informed of the boundaries of confidentiality at the beginning of data collection. If they gave information that indicated they or another person had come to harm, or were at risk of harm, then they would be told that this 'would not just be between us'. This would then be passed on to the relevant people.

Methods

Children's Research Advisory Group

The Children's Research Advisory Group (CRAG) was integral to my research, and for me an important building brick of participatory research. Input from the community of study, in this case autistic young people, can improve the quality of research methods and help transform qualitative methods into participatory working; albeit, this is not yet prevalent in the field (see Fletcher-Watson et al., 2019). The CRAG was a representative group of three autistic young people of similar age to the rest of the participants. They advised on the initial research design, specifically the methods used, and provided clarification on the aspects of educational experience that should be explored. The CRAG affirmed issues, such as teacher characteristics and peer relations, that, from experience and the literature, were already considered to be important. This helped me to develop research methods and instruments that were authentic, applicable, engaging and ultimately able to support the research aim and questions. As researchers in Scott-Barrett, Cebula and Florian (2018) suggest, researchers should exercise caution against imposing their adult assumptions about how children and young people want to participate and communicate. Children and young people have 'significant expertise to contribute' (Parsons, Sherwood and Abbott, 2016, p.141).

Through the use of guiding questions, the CRAG discussed each of the proposed data collection activities. These are summarised below, first to provide context for the methodology chosen and, second, to show the benefits of using a CRAG.

Session 1

I highlighted that the CRAG had a role to play in making the research better by giving advice on its methods and approaches and about what would work best with other young people (the materials, instruments, activities and language used). I reiterated that members were volunteers and could withdraw from the CRAG if they wished.

What aspects of education are important to explore? The CRAG chose teachers, their classmates, the lessons and the school.

What are the best ways to help children share their views? The CRAG suggested that a range of different short activities might be useful to keep participants interested and help get as much information as possible. Two of the CRAG members said they liked to chat about things informally and that talking about various issues would be a good way to explore them. I mentioned recording the chats (interviews) with a Dictaphone. They asked what this was – and were shown it. All three said it might make people nervous at the start. I suggested that the alternative would be me making lots of notes and they thought that this would be more distracting. I suggested that each participant could have time using the Dictaphone with me and they thought this was a good idea to help reassure and put participants at ease.

Session 2

They felt the interview would be the most intensive aspect of the research and that they would like to have it completed first. The CRAG considered the following questions (the questions were mind mapped and I provide a summary for each):

1 *What are the benefits of a group interview?*

- It might encourage more children to give ideas by seeing others providing ideas.
- It may not be as intense having other participants there.

2 *What are the drawbacks of a group interview?*

- Some children may feel embarrassed talking about experiences in front of other pupils.
- Some people might mess about and disrupt it.
- The group might have members missing sometimes.

3 *What are the benefits of a one-to-one interview?*

- It could be easier to arrange times to meet.

- Children might be happier to talk more with fewer people there.
- It would be quieter.
- Breaks can happen more easily.
- More privacy, especially if sensitive issues were discussed.

4   *What are the drawbacks of a one-to-one interview?*

- It might be very 'full on' (intense).

5   *Which format would work best?*

- All three agreed that one-to-one would be best.

I also asked the CRAG members for their thoughts on a semi-structured approach. I highlighted that the interview could also take place using a very structured schedule or no set structure at all. After a brief discussion all felt a semi-structured approach was best to keep participants focused yet help them to explore other issues that might not come up otherwise.

Do any of the interview questions not make sense? We went through each question (without all the potential prompts) to check if they made sense. No issues were raised. The CRAG members thought that the proposed activities included during the interview were useful and would probably help participants think about the issues more.

Have you any questions to add to the interview schedule? The CRAG members couldn't think of any other questions to add. I also asked whether they thought being given the interview schedule beforehand would help children with coming up with answers. They agreed that this would help.

Session 3

I explained that this session would focus on the other activities and that I wanted to provide a variety of ways for capturing the experiences and opinions of participants. I again highlighted the members' right to withdraw from the CRAG if they so wished.

We first focused on the activities included in the interview schedule (I detail these later).

Activity sheet A – What do you think about school? The CRAG liked the idea of giving a score out of ten. I asked why and they said it was easy to understand.

Activity sheet B – In school I am usually… Choose 5 feelings. The CRAG felt the range of feelings and the use of emojis were good. One member asked for clarification on feeling unwell (was it nervous sick or like a tummy bug). I explained that it was more like nervous/anxious –

I was then aware of the need to explain this to participants. One asked about confident and I explained it was about feeling able to do things and not being frightened of trying. They agreed that the range of feelings was suitable but that maybe going through these two with all children would be useful to make sure they knew what they meant.

Activity sheet C – 'More children with autism are being made to go to mainstream schools' – what do you think about this? The CRAG thought this was important to discuss but that some may not want to write or draw and rather give spoken answers.

Activity sheet D – What does school inclusion mean to you? The CRAG again thought this was a good thing to discuss but that it was a very hard question and some children might not have anything to say, or may not understand this. Two said it was still worth using but one was not so sure.

Beans and Pots activity – I explained that for each statement the participants would vote 'true', 'not sure' or 'not true' by putting a ball in a pot. I suggested that another way would be to have these in a list with tick boxes (take a survey). They said the beans and pots activity was best. I initially had 20 statements but they suggested reducing this – I reduced it to 17.

Diamond Ranking activities – They asked me to explain this as they had never done this type of activity before. I explained that these activities would involve participants arranging nine aspects of school that are supportive and nine aspects which may act as barriers to education in levels, from most to least (I discuss this further below). One CRAG member suggested that it might be good to have a practice. I suggested ranking food preferences and they agreed this would work.

A Good Teacher and a Bad Teacher – I explained that participants are free to draw on the outline and write descriptions/feelings on it. I explained that I would have a list of words available to help aid participants. They felt this was a good activity but that drawing might not appeal to all; again emphasising the need to be flexible and support multiple modes of communication.

My ideal school would look like this… – I explained that, after drawing the ideal school, I would ask for an explanation from each participant. Two CRAG members expressed that some may enjoy drawing, but one said they would not be so keen.

Semi-structured interview and building rapport

Kvale's (1996) criteria for being a successful interviewer remained foremost in my mind – being gentle, prepared, sensitive and focused. I sat at eye level with the participants, at an angle, but was mindful not to seek eye contact throughout as many autistic children have difficulty with such contact. I used humour to create a relaxed atmosphere, but, as my teaching experience with autistic children has affirmed, I avoided creating 'fake' friendships. During an interview there is a continued need for building rapport and maintaining relationships with children. This began in advance of data collection. I held an introductory session with science experiments with participants in the study hub and an introductory video, as discussed. I reinforced this rapport by showing genuine interest in a participant's thoughts and experiences. I used verbal affirmation to support non-verbal cues, particularly as autistic children can experience difficulties with non-verbal communication such as facial expressions, body language and vocal intonation (Attwood, 2007).

Autistic children can be trusting from the outset when traditional social boundaries are removed (Scott-Barrett, Cebula and Florian, 2018). In my case, trust was earned through building rapport and providing information that was meaningful. I wanted to ensure that they felt their experiences were going to be given genuine interest (or audience, according to Lundy's model). This was confirmed informally by three of the young people, who said they enjoyed the experience and that they felt they were finally being listened to without judgement or being told they were wrong. The vividness of the participants' narratives demonstrates this (see Chapters Six to Eight).

Recognising silence

Silences are a powerful and important feature in the discussion of voice (Cook-Sather, 2006). They can be used to convey additional information (Lewis, 2010), such as an unwillingness to respond, but do not always mean a young person does not understand. Lewis (2010, p.19) advocates that the purpose of silence – how it is recorded and the researchers' 'epistemological position in relation to the interpretation of silence' – should be considered. For me silences are an important aspect of voice, and, alongside body language, can indicate a young person's wellbeing. Voice is not limited to what is spoken. Throughout the interviews and the entire research process I actively listened to all communications. I recorded silences and participants' distinctly different body languages to ensure that every aspect of voice was accounted for. With a complete picture of voice I could be more aware of the impact a question or topic was having on the participant and how they were feeling.

Collecting the data: participatory methods

Participatory methods were used to gain 'authentic' knowledge about children's subjective realities, to help support the participants in expressing their experiences by providing them with appropriate and engaging opportunities in a safe and inclusive environment (Lundy and McEvoy, 2012). They were also used to maximise research accessibility and ensure that children's participatory rights could be exercised by offering multiple means of representation. Offering participatory methods helped mitigate anxiety associated with expressing experiences verbally, and supported participants 'to access and represent different levels of experience' (Bagnoli, 2009, p.547; see Komulainen, 2007). These approaches also provided a joint focal point for researcher and participant, thus reducing reliance on face-to-face verbal communication, widening opportunity for participation and also reducing pressure for participants to respond to direct questioning. The use of participatory activities also bolstered the continued rapport developed with the young person, ultimately positively influencing the entire research process and data quality.

Using drawings

I considered drawing to be an appropriate approach for those who may experience difficulties with communication, and it is described as more closely representing thought for children by offering a non-verbal mode of expression (Dockett and Perry, 2005). Participants were asked to provide explanations of any drawings they produced – a draw-and-tell technique (Driessnack, 2006). Drawing can shift attention from the adult researcher, placing the child in the position of expert which can result in rewarding non-verbal data (Driessnack, 2006; Leitch, 2008). This again reduces the inference of correctness and helps redress the balance of power. Flexibility gave participants the freedom to choose the medium for sharing their thoughts, particularly as autistics often 'think in pictures' (Attwood, 2007, p.236). However, despite most children being familiar with drawing activities, alternatives were offered for those who may have an aversion to drawing (verbal descriptions or writing – including me as a scribe). Drawing enabled creativity and provided an alternative and supportive means of representation, but did not constitute an arts-based approach. I now outline each participatory activity.

Beans and Pots activity

Participants moved around to each of 17 statements (Table 5.1 below) and decided whether each was 'true', 'not true', or if they were 'unsure'. These options were visually supported with thumbs up, thumbs down and a question mark (see Figure 5.4), as ticks and crosses could have inferred correctness. Participants placed a personalised polystyrene ball into the pot to indicate their preference for each statement. I self-produced these statements as another method to explore the young people's school experience, beyond the semi-structured interview.

For ease of organisation and to help with analysis I recorded the chosen response on a data collection sheet.

Diamond ranking

Diamond ranking, as an interactive research tool, helps young people construct and interpret information (Clark, 2012). Three diamond ranking activities were developed: the first acted as a capacity-building exercise to practise using the activity by ranking different foods into levels of preference; the second focused on ranking nine aspects of school I felt were important and how supportive and enabling these were; and the third sought information on potential worries about school that could act as barriers to accessing education in mainstream school. Again, these were developed by me. Some of the aspects and features to be ranked, such as 'being bullied' or 'the classroom environment being too noisy and busy', were reflective of the reviewed literature on educational experience (see Table 5.2). The most important feature goes at the top of the

Table 5.1 Beans and Pots activity statements

I enjoy going to school	I have friends at school
I would attend a school for only children with ASD/autism	People notice when I am good at something
Teachers like me the way I am	People at school are friendly to me
There is an adult I can talk to if I have problems	Teachers want to support me
I wish I was at a different school	Other children like me the way I am
I feel different from other children here	I feel happy being at school
School makes me feel anxious	I feel scared at school
I feel excited going to school	I feel accepted in school
I feel included in school	

Figure 5.4 Beans and Pots activity

Table 5.2 Diamond ranking aspects

Supportive aspects of school	Potential worries about school
Having friends at school	Being bullied
My teacher understanding me for who I am	Being in school for the whole day (9am-3pm)
My teacher being trained in autism	My teacher
Being able to take breaks when I need them	Too many peers (children in my class)
Class work based around my interests	Homework
Having a small class (less than 10 pupils)	Being in the playground
Having a quiet safe place to go when feeling anxious or stressed	Not having a quiet space to go to when stressed
Having visual schedules and visual supports	Break time and lunch time
Having activities to do at break time and lunch time	The classroom environment being too noisy and busy

diamond, followed by the next two and then a middle three ideas, down to the single least important aspect (Figure 5.7). This allowed 'levels' of importance to be created that did not rely heavily on degrees of feeling, such as scales ranging from 'strongly agree' to 'strongly disagree', especially as autistic children (as with others) may need some explanation of what different degrees of feeling mean (Honeybourne, 2015).

Good teacher, bad teacher

Participants were given two generic outlines of a figure and were invited to draw, add words, feelings and descriptions to these to describe the characteristics of a good and a bad teacher. Words were provided on stickers for pupils who do not like writing or need support with word finding (no one opted to use these).

Me at school

Participants were invited to produce a drawing of themselves at school. Again, this afforded participants the opportunity to demonstrate their feelings and experiences beyond the spoken word. They were encouraged to add written descriptors and asked to orally describe their drawings. Asking SEND pupils to draw a picture of themselves in the classroom can be an enlightening and informative way to seek their perceptions and feelings of their experiences.

Design your own school activity

This activity allowed participants to freely express, through drawing, what kind of school they would like (the ideal school). Murray and Lawson (2007) suggest that autistic children should be involved in designing their learning zones; this activity allowed them to give opinions on the entire school learning zone.

Inclusion activities

Two activities asked participants to discuss inclusion. The first simply asked the young people to respond to the statement 'More children with autism are being made to go to mainstream school' and young people could write, draw or describe this. The second asked them what inclusion means to them.

Table 5.3 presents a snapshot of matters I considered prior to and during my research (similar is presented in Goodall, 2018a).

Reflexivity and my position as practitioner-researcher

Bryman (2012, p.393) offers a description of reflexivity in which 'social researchers should be reflective about the implications of their methods, values, biases and decisions for the knowledge of the social world they create'. However, it is impossible to eliminate the influence of the

Table 5.3 Snapshot of methodological considerations

Consideration	Action taken
Auditory processing difficulty	The mother of one participant, Sarah-Jane, informed me that she experienced auditory processing difficulties. An initial email interview took place and was followed up with a face-to-face meeting. This reduced pressure associated with real-time responding to the initial interview questions. Autistic individuals have diverse cognitive processing speeds (Grandin, 2009). To aid processing I gave time after asking a question and repeated questions verbatim, as changing the language/wording may then present a slightly different question. I was also conscious of continually asking myself the question, 'what is the young person making of this?' (see Westcott and Littleton, 2005).
Responding and expressing themselves fully if under pressure	Honeybourne (2015, p.59) discusses how open-ended questions may not help in eliciting an accurate view of experiences as 'many can struggle to express themselves fully, especially if under pressure to respond quickly'. To overcome this, and as advised by the CRAG, the interview schedule was provided in advance to allow participants time to form their responses and to clarify anything about which they were unsure. However, the young people in my study responded well to open questions with the support of prompts. Initial questions helped relax and settle participants. These centred around non-research topics, such as their favourite movie. Participants were offered the opportunity to use the Dictaphone to ask me questions from a set list, again to reduce anxiety associated with the research situation and also to help with power-imbalance. Young people were also provided with a 'pass' and 'break' card to use throughout, alongside them being positioned close to the door for easy exiting if required.

(Continued)

Table 5.3 (Cont.)

Consideration	Action taken
Question style and interview schedule	Double or leading questions, questions containing too many negatives or overly complicated language were avoided (Honeybourne, 2015). Closed questions and prompts were also used to help the participants. I also asked for their responses to various statements across different activities, such as 'beans and pots'. Mauthner (1997) suggests that interviews with children work best when structured around several activities, as I did. This helps reduce the intensity of a long interview.
Word finding difficulties and understanding	I asked participants to choose five feelings that they associate with their time in school (with flexibility to add their own if they wanted). These also acted as prompts and visual supports to help initiate further discussion. Feeling words were supported visually by an emoticon to help with identifying and expressing emotions. These were laid out on chairs around the room, and on a single sheet if they would rather not move around. The participants were able to identify emotions and expand with detailed explanation and further descriptors of their own choosing. When scoring school out of ten, participants could see the numbers laid out on the floor. Jack and Wade enjoyed walking up and down the line of numbers while they thought. As noted above, one of the diamond ranking activities acted as a capacity-building exercise.

qualitative researcher (their biases), nor should it be his intention: he is central to the research and can provide a wealth of insight which can enrich the data. Reflecting on and understanding the influence and potential bias the individual researcher may have will help enhance the trustworthiness of qualitative research. Qualitative researchers are not disconnected from the research but are integral and are key research instruments for data collection and analysis.

As a practitioner-researcher with more than a decade of experience working closely with many autistic young people I have developed an understanding of the complexity of autism and the need for adaptive approaches to communicating with each participant; recognising the participants as individuals, rather than as one homogenous group because of their shared label of 'autism'. This knowledge and experience of building relationships was advantageous to method design and data collection, generating rich and meaningful data and arguably improving the research study – perhaps more so than would have been the case with a less-experienced researcher. For example, at the beginning of one data collection session one participant came into the room worked up, unsettled and boisterous (one of the pitfalls of data collection during a school day is that what has happened prior to the session may overflow into it). If I had had no working knowledge of the young person this could have been badly handled and resulted in a negative experience for both parties. However, knowing him well, and with gentle support, reassurance, affirmation, understanding and a listening ear for why he was upset he was able to regulate himself and settle. He was keen to continue with the session, once calm.

Approach to data analysis

Inductive or deductive framework for analysis

I followed an inductive approach, as is often used by qualitative researchers, to allow 'research findings to emerge from the frequent, dominant or significant themes inherent in raw data, without the restraints imposed by structured methodologies' (Thomas, 2003, p.2). I had to organise the data into meaningful categories, scrutinise these in a holistic way, and then communicate findings to others. I wished to avoid a deductive approach to analysis, as this is more closely aligned to quantitative experimental and hypothesis testing methods and can obscure key themes that could be uncovered through inductive approaches (Thomas, 2003).

Thematic analysis

Thematic analysis is a method of identifying, analysing and reporting patterns (themes) within qualitative data. Thematic analysis was used with interview transcripts to support steps two and three of inductive analysis discussed above. I found Braun and Clarke's (2006; 2014) six phase process for thematic analysis most useful. However, I was mindful that following the process step-by-step, like a recipe, does not always guarantee a good outcome.

Each interview was carefully transcribed verbatim and included the question asked, the response given and accompanying notes on participant silence and changes in body language. Careful transcription enhanced the dependability of analysis and also allowed me, the researcher, to become more familiar with the data (Braun and Clarke, 2014). This also influenced my decision against using qualitative analysis software, as it allowed me to be immersed in the interview data at each stage (from transcription to analysis). Although the use of an analysis package could have eased the burden of handling such large volumes of data, for me, as sole researcher, there was a risk of removing the 'craft element' (James, 2012, p.564) – the creation of a rich tapestry of data.

Phase 1: Becoming familiar with the data – which came from reading through interview transcripts several times before systematically highlighting or adding written comments to salient parts of the data. I looked through all other data to get a general overview of what the young people were sharing and combined data from various activities into more manageable documents.

Phase 2: Generating initial codes – coding reduces data to a more manageable feat. Figure 5.6 shows a small excerpt from an interview transcript with a young person (Ro) in my study.

Phase 3: Searching for themes – a theme is described as representing some level of patterned response or meaning within the data set (Braun and Clarke, 2006). After the initial coding (using the comments feature of Microsoft Word) I moved to identify themes within the data by grouping codes under descriptive headings. I was mindful that I had approached data collection based on broad research questions – around themes – relating to the participant's past educational experiences, present experiences and thoughts on the ideal school. I physically manipulated codes into initial themes; these were the printed comments applied in Microsoft Word. I underestimated the length of time this phase would take.

Phase 4: Reviewing themes – I checked the themes in relation to the coded data and the entire data set – reflecting on the actual verbatim data provided – to start building up a web, or map, of themes and identifying how they interconnect.

Phase 5: Defining and naming themes – the three themes, with subthemes, became apparent from the analysis of the data. These are outlined in Figure 5.7 and also form Chapters Six to Eight.

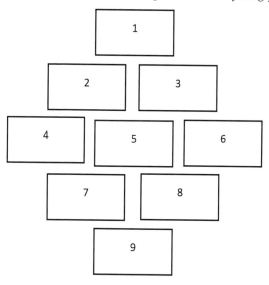

Figure 5.5 Template for the diamond ranking activities

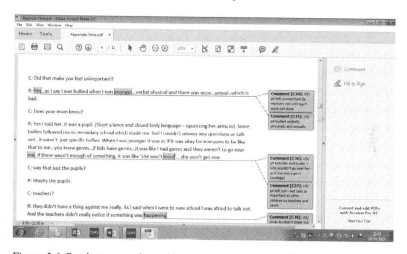

Figure 5.6 Semi-structure interview transcript excerpt with codes using Microsoft Word

Phase 6: Producing the report. What became evident was that data analysis does not follow a linear path but is a recursive process, with much going back before going forward. By taking a short break (several days) I allowed the data to breathe. When I re-immersed myself I was able to develop the interconnections between themes more clearly.

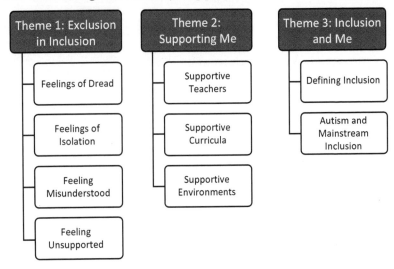

Figure 5.7 Main themes and sub-themes

Word clouds

A word cloud (as presented in Chapter Six) is one means by which to summarise and visually present the frequency of an aspect of data, such as the feelings chosen by participants to describe how they felt at mainstream school. The greater the frequency of a feeling, the larger font it has within the word cloud. This allows for quick identification of the most frequently used words, thereby providing instant understanding of a selection of text. Word clouds are a useful method in exploratory qualitative data analysis in social research, allowing for quick visualising of some general patterns (McNaught and Lam, 2010). I used Wordle, a web-based provider, to create these (http://www.wordle.net/create).

Analysis of drawings

The drawings and accompanying narratives were analysed from a meaning-making perspective, seeking out recurring themes, rather than being appraised on an aesthetic or cognitive basis. It is recognised that 'the interpretation belongs with the child, rather than the researcher' (Dockett and Perry, 2005, p.515), and listening to the accompanying verbal narratives helps ensure that adult interpretations are not imposed in understanding the drawings (Clark and Moss, 2001).

I end with a brief discussion of how I enhanced trustworthiness and authenticity.

Trustworthiness and authenticity in qualitative research

Guba's (1981) model provides a usable framework in which trustworthiness is the goal, rather than validity. This is achieved by demonstrating credibility (how confident the researcher is in the truth of the research findings), transformability (how the researcher demonstrates that the findings are applicable to other contexts), dependability (the extent that the study could be repeated by other researchers and how much detail is provided by the researcher to allow this) and confirmability (the neutrality of the researcher in ensuring the findings are those of the participants, accounting for potential researcher bias). Checklists exist to guide researchers in reaching these four tenets of trustworthiness. One such checklist (McMillan and Schumacher, 2006) highlights several approaches, including:

- The use of multi-method strategies to allow for data triangulation in collection and analysis. I used a range of activities to approach a similar topic in order to explore multiple perceptions to clarify meaning and verify the repeatability of interpretation. For instance, statements within the 'beans and pots' activity, interview questions, aspects of the 'diamond ranking' activity and asking the young person to draw themselves in mainstream school concerned educational experience and school improvement;
- Verbatim accounts of experiences given by participants; precise detailed descriptions recorded. I not only recorded their voices with a Dictaphone, but I transcribed each interview myself. I also noted any moments of silence or notable changes in body language during the interview to capture the entirety of their voice (see Table 5.3 on p. 75);
- Informal accuracy checks with participants during data collection (participant verification). Understanding was checked sensitively during interviews, questions were reconfigured as required and follow-up prompts were used. Interview data were authenticated by returning to the participants to go through the transcript. Verbal or written descriptions accompanied drawings to avoid misinterpretation of the data by me, as researcher.

In order to enhance the trustworthiness and authenticity of the interview data, as discussed above, careful consideration was given to question design and other activities used to ensure that my preconceived thoughts on the educational experiences of autistic children did not direct children to answers I wanted. This, and the use of the CRAG, enhanced the trustworthiness of the research. As discussed, their voices influenced the issues of education to explore and the methods used.

Concluding comments

'Participatory research enables meaningful input from autistic people in autism research' (Fletcher-Watson et al., 2019, p.943). This chapter demonstrated that recognising potential research 'dilemmas' or challenges, and considering aspects of methodology to overcome these in a participant-centric way, not only enhances the credibility and trustworthiness of research but can also support and advance children's rights, their position as experts in their own lives and, in turn, lead to deeper and more authentic understanding of the lived experiences and voices of autistic young people. Fletcher-Watson et al. (2019) propose two broad categories for advancing autism participatory research, centred on supportive environments and methodological considerations. The former includes aspects discussed in Chapter One, such as changing the language we use to describe autism and autistic participants in research, while the latter involves considering the methods used, how we ask interview questions and how we redress power imbalance and support 'voice' through multiple means of representation.

Chapters Six to Eight present the educational experiences of the 12 autistic young people, their thoughts on school improvement and what inclusion means to them. The rich and often emotive testimonies demonstrate the insightful narratives these young people have to share when supported to do so.

6 The educational experiences of autistic young people, from their perspectives

Introduction

Across the remaining chapters you will hear from 12 autistic young people aged 11–17 years, including two girls. In this chapter I present their many and varied educational experiences, mainly in mainstream but also in the Alternative Education Provision or study hub they attended. First, I provide a brief methodological overview of my Doctoral study to contextualise the remaining chapters.

Methodological overview

Research Perspective: Children's Rights Based Approach – Rights Respecting Qualitative – participatory	Approach and Methods: Rights based Children's Research Advisory Group Participatory activities (including writing and drawing, diamond ranking and beans and pots) and semi-structured interviews; analysed qualitatively (thematic analysis).
Research Aim: To explore the educational experiences of autistic young people, their thoughts on educational improvement and inclusion.	
Setting and participants: Twelve autistic young people aged 11–17 years attending an Alternative Education Provision (AEP) and others outside the AEP.	Ethical Considerations: Power relations, researcher bias, informed consent, voluntary participation, and protection from harm (including confidentiality and research space).

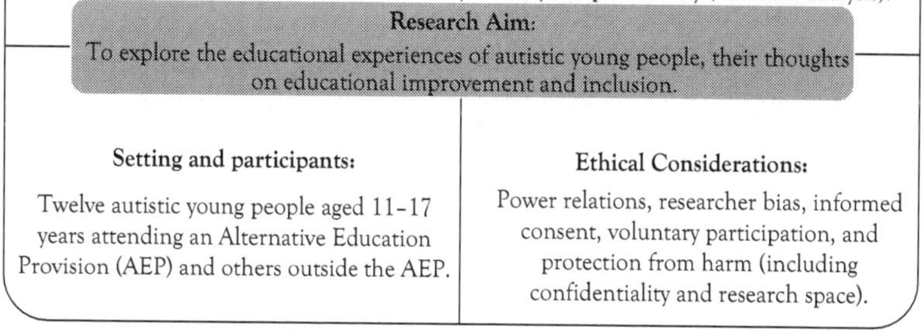

Figure 6.1 Methodological overview

Participants

Purposive convenience sampling was used. All 15 autistic young people within the AEP where I teach, and all seven children of the committee members of a 'voluntary study hub', were invited to participate to provide opportunity for each young person to take part. Seven boys attend the AEP (having come from mainstream schools): Jim (aged 14:1), Joe (aged 15:2), Lee (aged 13:10), Robert (aged 16:4), Stephen (aged 15:5), Thomas (aged 15:4) and Timmy (aged 15:7). Five of the participants were home schooled as a result of struggling with attending mainstream provision even on a part-time basis: these children attend a study hub. These are Dan (aged 11:3), Jack (aged 12:3), Ro (female, aged 16:1), Sarah-Jane (female, aged 17:0) and Wade (aged 13:11, attending mainstream on a part-time basis). Table 6.1 provides a key to identifying the activity and participant the extracts of data came from.

Table 6.1 Key to identifying data extracts

Code	Meaning
I	Semi-structured interview
p	Page number of semi-structured interview transcript
C	Sheet C: 'More children with autism are being made to go to mainstream school' – what do you think about this?
D	Sheet D: What does school 'inclusion' mean to you?
MeAtSch	Me At School activity
MyIdSch	My Ideal School activity
GtBt	Good Teacher, Bad Teacher activity
W	Wade
SJ	Sarah-Jane (female) (SJa indicates transcript 'a' and SJb indicates transcript 'b')
Ro	Ro (female)
D	Dan
J	Jack
Jo	Joe
Ji	Jim
Ti	Timmy
Th	Thomas
L	Lee
S	Stephen
R	Robert
Examples	I/D/p1 = Semi-structured interview, Dan, page 1 of transcription

Educational experiences

Participants described a wide range of educational experiences, most from multiple educational placements and some from across primary and secondary levels (such as Sarah-Jane, who experienced six placements in total). They all discussed negative experiences of mainstream education relating to the school environment, teachers, the curriculum and peers – these, to varying degrees, contributed to the feeling of exclusion in inclusion. As I discuss, islets of positive experiences were provided within individual education settings, particularly within the AEP or study hub that participants attended at the time of data collection.

I have arranged responses as sub-themes beneath the overarching theme of 'exclusion in inclusion'. These interrelated sub-themes, relating to emotional and psychological wellbeing, are: feelings of dread; feelings of isolation; feeling unsupported; and feeling misunderstood. First, I provide an overview of feelings chosen to describe participants' mainstream educational experiences (Figure 6.2).

For comparison, Figure 6.3 (presented previously in Goodall, 2019, p.20) shows the feelings of the seven boys from the AEP regarding their AEP experiences. The mean score out of ten for mainstream was 3.6 and 7.7 for the AEP.

Feelings of dread

Dread became a common thread after I grouped data under the codes of 'distress', 'stressful environment', 'before the school day' and 'school impact'. There was a preponderance of responses relating to the sub-theme of dread across various data collection activities. Eleven of the 12

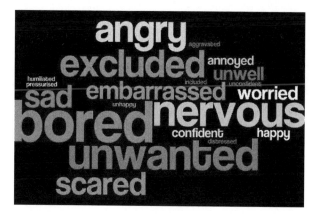

Figure 6.2 Word cloud – feelings chosen to describe mainstream school

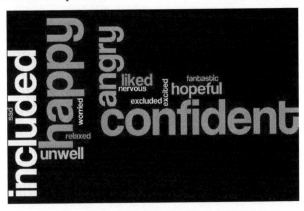

Figure 6.3 Word cloud – feelings chosen to describe the AEP

participants completed the 'beans and pots' activity, of whom nine chose 'true' in response to 'school makes me feel anxious'; with five also indicating they felt scared at mainstream school. Eight chose 'untrue' for the statement 'I enjoy going to school', with three choosing 'unsure'. Similarly, ten chose 'untrue' for the statement 'I feel happy being at school' and nine did not feel excited going to school.

When responding to the statement 'I wish I was in a different school' only six chose 'true'. Sarah-Jane, who had very negative mainstream school experiences, chose 'unsure'. Ro, who, like Sarah-Jane, described many negative aspects and experiences of mainstream school, chose 'untrue' but clarified this by saying, 'I wished I wasn't there at the time, but didn't think another school would be better'. Wade was 'unsure' if he wished he were at a different school. He described how he wished the school would change to support him rather than him having to change. He would like to go to a school where he was safe, happy and felt wanted and included.

Several participants described the negative impact of mainstream school on their wellbeing at school and difficulties that they experienced in getting through the school day, as the following extracts illustrate.

> My time at primary school was very stressful. At secondary school, the problems and difficulties got worse (I/SJa/p1). You know what? I am not doing this [secondary school] anymore. I am physically, mentally and emotionally drained … I am done with this. Talking about it [mainstream school] makes me angry … and upset (I/SJb/p9).

> School was always awful (I/D/p1). In fact, I went through a bit of severe depression. I wished I was dead. I have to go to school [sad expression] … I was always dreading it (I/D/p4).

School was toxic (I/W/p1) … this is an underestimation … it was hell. At X [school name removed] I was borderline suicidal (I/W/p7).

School was hell (I/J/p1). I tried to run away from school. It was too much (I/J/p3).

Several spoke of apprehension, dread and the despair they felt before going to school:

I never felt excited, always dread. This is how I felt about a normal school day and how it would go. I would not want to get up, I wouldn't want to open my eyes. I would wish I was still asleep (I/D/p4). It was a never-ending cycle, every day … I dreaded the repeat of that cycle (I/D/p5).

I would feel distressed, scared and upset [before school] (I/W/p3).

The night before school I would put off going to sleep to put off school as much as possible … staying in bed as long as possible and getting up at the last minute. The bus was stressful enough … have I missed the bus, what if there are no seats. I had a big thing about people looking at me and being judged (I/Ro/p3).

I was worried about going into school the next day [sad facial expression] … I fucking hated the school! I got sent home or ran away all the time … I hated them (I/Jo/p4).

Young people elaborated on the source of their stress and dread. These include factors within the school environment – such as auditory sensory overload, social anxiety and social pressure – arising from the unpredictability and sometimes overwhelming nature of the main-stream environment. In the 'diamond ranking' activity, 'the class environment being too noisy and busy' and 'being in school for the whole day' were ranked top worries overall.

I was very stressed trying to cope with the noise, the large class sizes, the constant changing of classrooms (I/SJa/p1). Secondary school was very large with lots of corridors (I/SJa/p5). Asperger's made it very difficult for me to cope with life in a large secondary school; there was too much noise and too many people to deal with. It was awful moving to the next class. It was just swarmed with people (I/SJa/p8). I felt closed in and like I couldn't breathe as there were so many people. It was so dif-ficult being in there all day (I/SJb/p6).

Figure 6.4 Thomas at school

Wade echoed this feeling of being closed in and being overwhelmed by the noise and number of people. It was, he said, *too crowded, too noisy, the corridors were too small, the classrooms were too noisy* (I/W/p6). *There was too much noise making me more stressed* (I/W/p7).

Thomas drew an image of himself at school to illustrate his frustration (Figure 6.4). He also spoke of the build-up of stress throughout the day. He offered a description of this picture:

> This is me pulling my hair out as I am so stressed at teachers, the work and being suspended. (MeAtSch/Th) I felt really annoyed ... the stress of the day had built up (I/Th/p4). It was too overwhelming and every single class was really noisy (I/Th/p3). It is too crowded ... over crowded (I/Th/p11).

Jack drew himself at school (Figure 6.5). He explains:

> This is my depiction of hell – me crying, sad and lots of unexpected 'lava'. Lava is like more work coming when in school. School [in red] is shooting hell down at me. A top hat and monocle has been added to the figure of me so teachers can't recognise me and give me more work or hassle me. The red diagram of school doesn't wear a monocle as it is not posh enough, nor does it really see what is going on [indicating that school does not see Jack and his experiences of school] (MeAtSch/J).

Ro and Stephen spoke of the social pressure, the unknown and dread and despair felt at break and lunch times, in particular using the school cafeteria.

> The cafeteria ... the noise and business and if you don't have a clique [group] to sit with, people in your class would be like 'what are you

Me at School (draw and/or write)

Figure 6.5 Jack at school

doing here?' and it was so full with people. You had to find somewhere to sit every time. It was a new piece of pressure each time going in. I went through whole days without eating to avoid it (I/Ro/p2).

You couldn't go to the canteen or go to the toilet in peace. Everyone would chase you. Too many people. Too much noise and worry about what could happen next (I/S/p11).

Bullying

In the 'beans and pots' activity, seven participants selected 'true' to the statement 'other children like me the way I am' with regard to the AEP or study hub, but only one (Timmy) selected 'true' when referring to mainstream school. Further, only four participants selected 'true' to the statement 'people are friendly to me in school'. Unsurprisingly, therefore, several of the participants who chose 'untrue' or 'unsure' discussed being bullied by peers at mainstream. Wade, Ro, Sarah-Jane, Thomas and Stephen describe their experiences of being bullied:

The children were probably one of the worst things there. They would constantly bully you. I got kicked, pushed and punched. I have also had pupils make verbal sexual comments towards me (I/W/p2).

Wade illustrates his experiences and supplemented this with a verbal description (Figure 6.6):

> There was a weight on my shoulders all the time. Other pupils are shouting kill yourself, the most common slur. This made me suicidal ... teachers tried to help but it got too much (MeAtSch/W).

Sarah-Jane outlined her experiences:

> I was often made fun of by my peers when I got the answers wrong (I/SJa/p3). At [secondary school] pupils weren't very nice, they could be abusive for no reason (I/SJa/p5). I was called a geek or weirdo. They [peers] don't care (I/SJa/p8).

Sarah-Jane highlighted that peers don't wish to befriend her because of her disability:

> It is all about themselves and if you have a disability they don't want to know, they look down at you and think 'no, I am not going to be with her' (I/SJb/p5).

Figure 6.6 Wade at school

Ro was bullied in primary and secondary school.

> I was bullied when I was younger ... verbal, physical and there was once ... sexual ... which is bad. It was a pupil. [Short silence and closed body language – squeezing her arms in.] Some bullies followed me to secondary school which made me feel I couldn't answer any questions or talk out ... it wasn't just specific bullies. When I was younger it was like I had germs and they weren't to go near me (I/Ro/p4).

Thomas, who drew himself red faced, also spoke of being bullied: *They [pupils] were all assholes as they tried to pick on me for being different* (MeAtSch/Th).

Stephen also spoke of being bullied:

> People would go around and bully you. If you didn't please them you were going to get hit that day (I/S/p1). That is one of the reasons why I cracked up in school. The bullying made me angry (I/S/p2).

Stephen provided a drawing of himself at mainstream school (his real name has been redacted in Figure 6.7). Peers are shown to make

Figure 6.7 Stephen at school

fun of his shoes, he is called a tramp by one and Stephen has a sad expression on his face.

Feelings of isolation

To differing degrees the young people experienced social isolation (including loneliness and being an outsider), physical isolation, emotional isolation and academic isolation. Participants indicated these emanated from interactions between the young person, their peers, teachers, the teaching approaches used and a lack of support.

For some, social isolation and loneliness arose from having no close friends or no one to relate to despite making efforts to build relationships. In response to the statement 'I have friends in school', six of the young people did, however, indicate this was 'true'. Sarah-Jane and Ro not only indicated this statement was 'untrue' but stated that they were not sure what a friend is. The following extracts from Sarah-Jane and Ro describe their experiences of isolation and loneliness:

> I found that I had no close friends and no one to talk to. I felt very lonely and often found myself without anyone to play with (I/SJa/p1). I was often excluded by the girls in my class. I spent break and lunch time wandering around on my own. I had no one to sit with in class (I/SJa/p3). Despite making the effort to be friendly with the ones in my class, I was always left out and on my own (I/SJa/p4).

> I didn't really have anyone to hang out with [on arriving to school] so I went to the library, but sometimes it wasn't open so I just stood awkwardly outside the classroom (I/Ro/p3).

Ro drew herself at school (Figure 6.8). 'I was isolated and separate, in like a bubble of depression and anxiety … but I still felt the centre of attention with others looking at me and judging' (MeAtSch/Ro).

The following extracts highlight a lack of friendships, but also demonstrate that well-used – and seemingly harmless – classroom approaches can exacerbate feelings of social isolation. For instance, teachers asking pupils to 'find a partner' provided further, more overt, occasions for Sarah-Jane to feel isolated and alone; an issue that will be revisited in Chapter Eight.

> As usual, I had no one and I was made to pair up with the teacher. I felt so little having to stand there waiting to pair up with the teacher.

Figure 6.8 Ro at school

It was awful. [I suggested a strategy of teachers randomly selecting names from hats each time.] It would have stopped me feeling humiliated and little inside standing there on my own in the classroom. It kind of scars you. Mentally it didn't help me (I/SJb/p10).

In the second 'diamond ranking' activity participants, overall, ranked 'having friends' as the second most important supportive and enabling factor – Jim, Joe, Lee and Timmy placed it as the top factor. However, for Ro having friends was ranked as least important. In the interviews, some participants, including Ro, mentioned that they were happy spending time alone or that they didn't wish to develop potential friendships beyond the school gates.

Opportunities for social interaction and friendship building were curtailed for some by having to catch up on missed homework during break time, or by being physically isolated from peers, as Sarah-Jane, Thomas and Dan describe:

At primary school I was often kept in at lunch time to complete my work and this meant that I was even more isolated as I missed out on the chance to play with anyone at lunch time (I/SJa/p2). I felt even more isolated because of this (I/SJa/p3).

There was a room next to it [the classroom] where I was chucked in when angry. It didn't have a lock but there was no handle on the inside. The teachers would sit with a chair and hold the door closed. I would choose to go there sometimes when I was angry (I/T/p4).

I didn't get to see my friends at all. I wasn't able to see anyone. Sometimes I saw a couple, but not much as most of the time we were just doing work (I/D/p1). One day [silence for three seconds] ... [voice quivering a little] it is a day I won't ever forget for a long time. It was actually the last day I went to school. It was the thing that made me leave. I was trying to get out but they locked me in the classroom ... they wouldn't let me out. I tried to get out and then they were up at the door. I opened the door and then they slammed it and my fingers were almost slammed off. I was always stuck in there [the classroom] and I was only ever let out for a small time (I/D/p2). It was a nice classroom, but you can't enjoy a nice room if you ... and you are locked in it. I was isolated from everything (I/D/p3). Occasionally I got to see them [peers], one day every few weeks possibly (I/D/p6).

Sarah-Jane, Dan, Jack, Wade and Jim felt unwanted (by peers and teachers) and spoke of being an outsider who didn't belong. Most (except Jim, Robert, Timmy and Thomas) selected 'true' to the 'beans and pots' activity statement 'I feel different from other children here [mainstream]'.

I always felt stressed, anxious and out of place (I/SJa/p2). I tried to fit in with everyone but always felt that I was an outsider (I/SJa/p4). I felt hurt when excluded by 'friends' [she thought they were friends] from joining in with an activity or left out by them when they met up after school without me being invited to join them (I/SJa/p5). I didn't feel like I fitted in to school or society. I didn't know how to act ... I kept myself to myself and didn't speak to anyone. I felt they were like different people (I/SJb/p2).

I didn't belong ... I was mostly unwanted by the teachers (I/D/p3).

I feel like I didn't belong there (I/W/p1). I felt super different (I/W/p2) ... [and] feeling unwanted (I/W/p3).

I always feel like an outsider (I/Ji/p8).

Attempts were made by teachers to try to support Ro in making friends, but no true friendships resulted. *He* [teacher she liked] *tried to get other girls to play with me but once that year ended they would stop playing with me. I thought I had made friends* (I/Ro/p5).

Sarah-Jane felt isolated academically from peers within the classroom, left outside the learning of the classroom by teaching practices and, again as will be discussed later, by a lack of support. Sarah-Jane explains:

> I was always much slower to understand and always found that I was slower to finish my work (I/SJa/p2). I found it difficult to follow the lessons (I/SJa/p3). I was switched off. If the support was there I could have accessed the curriculum (I/SJb/p9). There was no differentiation in classwork or at home (I/SJb/p4).

Feeling misunderstood

Eleven participants spoke of teachers not understanding them, their needs or autism. As I explore in Chapter Seven, every young person suggested that understanding is a fundamental attribute of a good teacher. Sarah-Jane, Stephen, Jack, Wade and Thomas illustrate this:

> They didn't understand that I had a learning difficulty (I/SJa/p5). [Failing in education] was due to a lack of understanding of my difficulties (I/SJa/p6).

> [Feeling misunderstood by teachers] they just thought I was just being bad all the time (I/S/p1).

> Whenever I was annoyed they kept on at me and this made me more annoyed (I/J/p11).

> I felt like they didn't understand as much as I would have liked them to (I/W/p4).

> They [mainstream teachers] are not understanding of certain individuals and their needs (I/Th/p11).

For Sarah-Jane, as highlighted above, being asked to find a partner was a recurring example of teachers lacking understanding of her challenges. This resulted in Sarah-Jane being left on her own or having to pair with the teacher. Below, I present examples of how this lack of understanding can lead to feelings of not being supported. Sarah-Jane suggests teacher's stereotyped young people with Asperger's Syndrome.

> They [teachers] had images of how a child with Asperger's should behave. In my opinion it is as if I was stupid (I/SJb/p5).

For Ro, a lack of understanding and stereotyping extended to feeling patronised:

> For me there was one time a different assistant came with me ... she was very condescending ... 'this means this and this means this' ... it was very patronising and as if she was saying this poor wee child and her wee brain disability, she can't think for herself (I/Ro/p8).

Dan expressed a lack of understanding of his behaviour, manifesting in feeling judged by teachers:

> Every time I felt I couldn't keep myself together properly I felt like they were just looking down at me (I/D/p4). Teachers make it [school] worse, they don't understand what I am going through [volume increased] (1/D/p5).

Feeling unsupported

Of the 11 participants who completed the 'beans and pots' activity, seven chose 'untrue' to the statement 'teachers want to support me', with three choosing 'unsure'. Furthermore, participants were divided when asked to respond to the statement 'there is an adult I can talk to if I have problems', with six choosing 'true' and four choosing 'untrue'. Ro chose 'unsure' and elaborated by saying: *looking back there was, but at the time I couldn't approach them due to anxiety.* In comparison to mainstream school, all participants felt they had an adult to approach in the AEP or study hub. Further, when asked to respond to the statement 'teachers like me the way I am' (in mainstream), only Stephen chose 'true'. Ro extended her 'unsure' response by saying that teachers didn't pay enough attention to her for her to have an opinion and that she was invisible – an issue revisited below. With regard to the AEP or study hub, the majority (eight) said this statement was 'true'.

Every participant provided examples of feeling unsupported in mainstream. These feelings stemmed from teachers lacking flexibility to adapt their teaching approaches and the curriculum to meet the individual needs of the young person. Wade, Sarah-Jane, Lee, Thomas and Joe explain:

There was close to no support (I/W/p1). I wished they were more flexible (I/W/p5).

There were no allowances for me not being able to do it [auditory mental maths, despite Sarah-Jane having significant language processing and auditory working memory difficulties] (I/SJb/p2). There was no differentiation in classwork or at home (I/SJb/p4). They never gave work in smaller chunks (I/SJb/p1). You were just given the work and told to get on with it without help. It [mainstream school] is not about them adapting to you, but you adapting to them (I/SJb/p3).

I was stressed at the teachers as they wouldn't listen to me. They never tried to understand me and were more interested in academics or their lesson (MeAtSch/Th).

No flexibility [from teachers] (I/Jo/p2). I didn't get any support (I/Jo/p5).

For Jim, not being supported resulted in him truanting school:

I walked in and walked out half an hour later because the teachers were bastards (I/Ji/p3). They didn't try and change anything to help you out (I/Ji/p4).

Sarah-Jane, Ro, Stephen and Jack felt teachers simply did not care enough about them to offer adequate support; they felt abandoned and unnoticed. They felt less important than other children who did not face the same challenges.

They [mainstream teachers] just kind of abandoned people who had problems (I/SJb/p1). They [teachers] didn't care (I/SJb/p8). I never felt supported. I never got help (I/SJb/p7). Teachers just focus on normal children; it probably looks good and is better for results and all that (I/SJb/p11). Excuse my language, it makes me feel pissed off at them, really pissed off and they did nothing to help me. They made me feel worse. [Short pause] ... I was so unhappy (I/SJb/p9).

They [mainstream teachers] didn't really care about how I felt (I/S/p1).

No one really made any attempt to ask about how I was doing. They [teachers] didn't really notice. As I was quieter they put me with the problem children for group stuff. I didn't talk out much, they must have assumed I was okay with it (I/Ro/p2). If there wasn't enough of something, it was like [teachers would say] 'she won't mind' ... she won't get one (I/Ro/p4). It was a mainstream school, and you know ... [short pause] there isn't much focus on individual children. I was quiet and during exams I was meant to get extra time, but I had to tell the teachers this repeatedly. This was very nerve wracking for me (I/Ro/p1).

Wade resigned himself to 'failure': *I would ask them for help and they wouldn't care* (I/W/p5). *I feel if I had have been taken care in the right way I could have done something good* (I/W/p7).

From his experience, Jack offered a short description of bad teachers: *They* [bad teachers] *are 'dead inside' and don't care about me as a person or how well I do* (Gt/Bt/J). This quote highlights the obtuseness of these teachers to the needs and personalities of students, which, as the 'exclusion in inclusion' theme exemplifies, impacts negatively on them.

Ro also explained how the Special Educational Needs Co-ordinator, the person appointed to oversee support for those with additional needs, was unapproachable:

> The special needs consultant in my school ... she was stern and unapproachable and overall not a pleasant person to be around. She wouldn't take you seriously at all (I/Ro/p5).

Aside from the above examples of not being supported, other associated feelings and experiences emerged, including being forgotten about, experiencing mistrust, feeling unfairly treated, feeling pressured, lacking choice and feeling controlled.

Timmy felt controlled and trapped by mainstream school, changing the title of the activity page to read 'me at jail' instead of 'me at school'. He illustrated these feelings (Figure 6.9):

Timmy offered a verbal explanation of his drawing: *I am trapped. I had no control, everything's in the school's control. I was bored and sad. I felt like an animal with no choice* [pause], *always controlled* (MeAtSch/Ti).

He extends this further in the 'good teacher, bad teacher' activity: [A bad teacher] *wants everyone to be the same and ignores individuality* (GtBt/Ti).

Timmy expanded on these experiences during the semi-structured interview:

> The fact they [teachers] gave you two choices ... it was too much pressure and was about their control over me (I/Ti/p2). They

Figure 6.9 Timmy at school

[teachers] were forceful telling me what to do. I learnt a really important lesson for life, if you are waiting for something [the end of the school day] don't count the time (I/Ti/p3).

Joe and Ro described experiences that led to feelings of mistrust of some teachers:

One day in school they [teachers] tried to tell me he [social worker] wasn't there ... he was there and they told me he wasn't. So I ran (I/Jo/p7).

The head of year, whenever I was out of school for stress and a nervous breakdown ... phoned home and then began gossiping to other teachers even though it was meant to be a private thing. Gossiping in front of students nonetheless, breaking my trust (I/Ro/p2).

Ro and others, namely Jim, Joe, Lee and Thomas, spoke of being unfairly treated and punished. Ro spoke of fear:

I had a huge fear of any kind of repercussion for anything. In school I feel crushed by every bit of stress and worry (I/Ro/p4).

> They [teachers] shout at you for no reason so I just walked out every day (I/Ji/p1).

Joe's start to secondary education was tainted from the outset by him not having a choice in school placement:

> I didn't have a choice of school. There were spaces. You know how you have to write down three schools. I wasn't allowed to put them down. Others in my primary class were allowed. I wasn't allowed (I/Jo/p6).

Some participants used the 'good teacher, bad teacher' activity to indicate further thoughts on their experience of unsupportive (or bad) teachers, with three mentioning that they felt teachers judged them based on past experiences with autistic young people. For instance, Ro, Joe and Wade explain:

> A bad teacher has preconceptions which impacts on how they treat pupils – judging all autistic children the same based on past experiences. They are inconsistent. This makes it hard to understand what is expected. Each day starts off worrying about how I will be treated or spoken to, making me scared of being shouted at (GtBt/Ro).

> Stereotypes me based on past experiences with other children with autism (GtBt/Jo).

> They use past experiences to judge current children (GtBt/W).

The impact of being unsupported is perhaps why most of the young people (nine) stated that mainstream school was, or had, failed them. Eight also spoke of having failed at mainstream school, with three being 'unsure'. Wade spoke of how he could have been a success if he had been cared for in mainstream school. Conversely, in relation to the AEP or study hub the ten who responded spoke of being successful and the setting being successful with them (see Goodall 2019).

Concluding comments

The young people have shared experiences that are many and varied. In the main, they spoke of the challenges they faced in mainstream schooling and the negative impact these had on their wellbeing and enjoyment of education. Most felt excluded; some by peers and others by teachers. They also discussed the stress, anxiety, dread and despair they felt before, during and after school. The unpredictability and overwhelming impact of the sensory and social environment – the 'chaos of the corridor' (Humphrey and Lewis, 2008a, p.38) – and the teachers (for some) underpin these negative feelings. As Connor (2000) expressed, anxiety can stem from an autistic person's need for predictability and routine. They often need to feel that they have control within their environment. Some participants noted that school was a place of control, with Timmy equating mainstream to jail. Most young people spoke of how they failed at mainstream school, and the young people were of the opinion that mainstream school had failed them. In the main, the young people feel unsupported and misunderstood by teachers in mainstream schools; some spoke of being unnoticed, being unwanted and not respected or supported as an individual.

Participants also discussed loneliness, isolation, being bullied and experiences of anxiety in mainstream; all of which are experiences congruent with the literature (for example, Brede et al., 2017; Hebron and Humphrey, 2014; Humphrey and Lewis, 2008a, 2008b; Humphrey and Symes, 2011; Poon et al., 2014; Sreckovic, Brunsting and Able, 2014). Bullying was a concern for some of the young people, an issue highlighted in Chapter Four (see for example, Humphrey and Symes, 2010; Hebron and Humphrey, 2014). Despite experiencing difficulties with social interaction, participants, in the main, expressed a desire for friendship and want to be with, and included by, peers – albeit this should not be forced, as some prefer time on their own. Other research studies also reflect this (see O'Hagan and Hebron, 2017). Several participants in this study provided instances of when they experienced physical, emotional and sexual bullying.

Participants experienced isolation by peers. If social isolation becomes the norm then autistic young people will struggle to be included in school and the wider community. They were also isolated physically and academically by some of the teaching practices and approaches used for curriculum delivery, such as being educated in isolation and being kept inside during break time to complete missed homework. Jack suggested this practice isolated him further from peers. Although this link between homework difficulties and subsequent social and physical isolation was not evident within the reviewed literature, Gibb et al. (2007) contend that both social and academic inclusion are important aspects of a child's educational experience. These practices exacerbate isolation, loneliness and feelings of being an outsider looking in – as documented by Sarah-Jane, who was regularly left alone when asked to find a partner in class. A lack of flexibility in teacher pedagogy is expressed by participants as a worry about school – a barrier to accessing the curriculum and to experiencing enjoyment of education. For Sarah-Jane, being treated in the same way as her peers through the use of auditory mental maths as a means of assessment proved exclusionary, as she had auditory processing difficulties. Participants did note that teachers lack time and training to be able to give the required support to them; an aspect considered a major factor for successful inclusion of autistic young people within literature exploring adult perspectives (for example, Hayes et al., 2013).

Participants did, however, offer examples of positive experiences they had had with individual mainstream school teachers who took an interest in them as a person and had expectations of them. Similarly, those participants who attended the AEP highlighted the personal connections teachers build with them, the interest that is taken in them and the in-depth knowledge of how to support them. Those who attended the study hub spoke of how the flexibility they have in working at their own pace, within their own routine and in their own space benefits them – giving the young people control over their learning environment, thus reducing the barrier of unpredictability as noted by participants in Humphrey and Lewis (2008a).

With regard to autistic girls, few studies have garnered their perspectives on how school has been for them, or how schools could be improved (see for example, Moyse and Porter, 2015; Sproston, Sedgewick and Crane, 2017). The experiences of Sarah-Jane and Ro presented here and in the next chapters enhance our understanding of how school is for this under-represented group.

7 Educational improvement, what autistic young people tell us

Introduction

By supporting young people, through engaging authentically with their voices and truly listening to what they have to say, we may hopefully be able to address the fractured nature of educational inclusion. Chapter Six presented the emotive descriptions of their educational experiences, and in this chapter I present thoughts, ideas and advice on how they, and other autistic pupils, can be supported better in mainstream education. Some of their advice is individual to them, emphasising the importance of not treating all as one homogenous group. Other suggestions would require wide systemic and cultural shifts within our education system. These are presented under the sub-themes 'supportive teachers', 'supportive curricula' and 'supportive environments'.

Supportive teachers

It is unsurprising, given the experiences outlined, that the young people emphasise personal attributes such as understanding, caring, kindness and flexibility as important aspects of a supportive teacher. The term understanding was preponderant across the data, particularly in the 'good teacher, bad teacher' activity which was used by participants to offer many attributes of a supportive (good) teacher. Most participants offered descriptors of bad teachers that reflected the experiences discussed in Chapter Six. However, Sarah-Jane offered a comprehensive description of a good supportive teacher – encapsulating elements of data from other participants – and how they would support an autistic young person (Figure 7.1) (see Goodall, 2018c).

Wade and Jack demonstrated pragmatism by reflecting their awareness of pressures experienced by teachers. Some of these, such as class sizes, alongside aspects of Sarah-Jane's suggestions, will be discussed below.

> *A good teacher is someone who takes time to listen.*
>
> *They understand the difficulties and problems that a young person with Asperger's syndrome/autism faces in a school.*
>
> *They realise that a person with ASD has sensory issues with noise, crowds etc and provides support and help when necessary.*
>
> *A good teacher realises that it can be difficult for someone with ASD to make friends.*
>
> *Provides an alternative to playground activities such as a quiet, reading/games room.*
>
> *A good teacher understands how to provide social activities to try to help the person with ASD to be an accepted member of the class/year group.*
>
> *They understand that planned activities might need changed to meet the particular needs of someone with ASD.*
>
> *A good teacher would provide a quiet area in class for those with ASD who need some time out and takes time to explain activities.*
>
> *Listens to parental concerns.*
>
> *I think a good teacher is someone who is patient, kind, understanding, helpful, considerate, calm and above all doesn't shout a lot.*

Figure 7.1 Sarah-Jane's description of a good supportive teacher

Stephen described aspects of the relationship and approach a good teacher would have with him:

> Understand me when I'm angry. Listen to me. Understand me for me. Don't hold grudges and be willing to work with me. Take an interest in me. They would look after me in school, give me boundaries and change how they teach so I can learn (GtBt/S).

Timmy also describes a good teacher as one who listens to him and is tolerant of his behaviours, but most importantly encourages him. He also notes that they would: *recognise my difficulties, but don't single them out* (GtBt/Ti).

Some participants also drew upon islets of support they experienced from mainstream teachers. For instance, Sarah-Jane spoke of supportive teachers in a primary school where she felt happiest. Here, teachers understood her needs and demonstrated this through the kindness they showed and the adaptations they made to the curriculum. Sarah-Jane gave this school a score of nine out of ten, compared to much lower scores for her other school placements. She explains:

They [teachers] were firm but kind and took their time to explain things that I didn't understand. They understood that I had some sort of learning difficulty and they would give me work that I was able to understand and complete (I/SJa/p3).

Ro spoke of two supportive teachers, one of whom had high expectations of her:

When I was enthusiastic about art she [Art teacher] took a liking to me. She expected a higher standard from me. It made me feel I had something to work for (I/Ro/p1).

Wade also spoke of a teacher he liked:

Out of everyone there I felt he [teacher] was the one who understood me the most. He got to know me and showed an interest (I/W/p4).

Likewise for Robert, Thomas and Stephen, personal attributes such as teachers being personable and showing an interest in them are important:

Yeah he got to know you personally and didn't just treat you like a number. Out of all the teachers he understood me the most really … he was really dead on (I/Rob/p2).

Being recognised as a person is important. The teacher has to want to get to know you (I/Th/p7).

They [teachers he liked] were kind, had a laugh, were fair (I/S/p1) … and understanding (I/S/p3).

Aside from teachers in mainstream, Lee, Robert and Stephen also drew on positive experiences they have had with teachers in the AEP (as found in Goodall, 2019). They noted teachers building personal connections, being fair, demonstrating flexibility, having understanding, having time for, and knowledge of, them and their individual difficulties. To summarise, Robert said:

The teachers are all really nice and understand you. Teachers know all about you and have an actual connection with you and want to help and want to know who you are [smile] and how to make things better for you (I/Rob/p4). I feel better about myself

> now and I feel more confident about getting on with my education
> (I/Rob/p6).

Dan, Thomas, Wade and Sarah-Jane offered advice to teachers. They mention training, but again emphasise understanding as key. The teacher's personal attributes are important to supporting them:

> If they [teachers] were understanding ... understanding me. A mixture of both [teacher training in ASD and positive personal attributes] would be useful. Having experience also matters (I/D/p6).

> They just made you feel they wanted to be teaching you (I/Th/p5).

> I think the best thing you can do is help someone. If you at least help someone you know you have done something good (I/W/p4). [Being a good teacher] depends on the person and not necessarily the training they have had. The children were a lot to deal with, but you can't change them. The teachers could at least try and change (I/W/p5).

> I just think teachers have to listen and understand [and they don't necessarily have to have training] (I/SJb/p4). I would have liked them [teachers] to have been more warm and friendly (I/SJb/p7).

Ro and Rob spoke of wanting teachers to care more about them than academic results:

> Actually start caring about the students rather than the results they give you. It is about teaching the children and not only caring for the results. Really knowing and paying attention to the children. If all you are going to do is stand there, recite material and look at results ... you know ... each child has their own individual needs (I/Ro/p7).

> It is more about a personal connection rather than a false connection over trying to get something [a qualification] (I/Rob/p5).

Very few young people referred to a lack of ASD training as a characteristic of a bad, or unsupportive, teacher in the 'good teacher, bad teacher' activity.

For Ro, ASD training was considered neither a good nor bad aspect of a teacher, with Joe indicating *training doesn't necessarily matter* (GtBt/Jo). Ro expanded on this in the semi-structured interview:

It [teacher training] makes some of the difference but it depends how it is used. It is a matter of taking the training and using it seriously and understanding that the child is their own person (I/Ro/p8).

Supportive curricula

Supportive teachers ensure their pupils have access to a curriculum that imparts knowledge and develops skills while also supporting emotional and social wellbeing. The strategies, approaches and adaptations used to deliver the curriculum can support pupil wellbeing and enable access to learning, or conversely young people can be left outside the learning of the classroom, becoming academically isolated, as mentioned earlier.

Dan and Wade discussed teachers who tried to implement strategies commonly used with autistic young people, but with little success. Dan told the teachers that schedules frustrate him, but, as he explains, one was used repeatedly. This exemplifies why strategies need to be considered on an individual basis and in consultation with the child – the 'one size fits all' approach will not work.

> I had a little schedule thing where I had to take things off and stick things on. It was so annoying I would rip all the things off it and say 'bye' and leave only the going home one. They would make me pick it all back up again and put it back on (I/D/p5).

Many participants suggested simple strategies and curriculum adaptations that they felt would have helped make their time at mainstream more successful. These range from simple adaptations in the delivery and content of the curriculum and in the teaching materials used. Sarah-Jane suggests:

> If they laid the work out step by step, maybe some pictures of what you have to do and how to lay out your answers would have helped me do really well. I can follow sums written down, but not just verbally. I don't know why they didn't do it (I/SJa/p4).

For Stephen, he needs instructions and tasks broken down as otherwise he has too much to do at once. *I can't do 'all this at once'… and I am cracking up* (I/S/p5).

Jack would benefit by verbal instructions being represented visually: *instructions visually supported would have helped* (I/J/p9).

Thomas and Dan (who is taught in a one-to-one situation) spoke of wanting a more interactive style of teaching and of having opportunities for socialising by working with peers:

> Include me more instead of just giving out text books. Making it more interactive and involving (I/Th/p2).

> Having some of my friends in the class or at least other people that I could try and make friends with them with breaks to talk to them or breaks away to work with them (I/D/p5).

Although only specifically noted by Dan, the use of a young person's interests to motivate and engage was important to all the participants collectively. In the 'diamond ranking' activity, 'class work based around interests' was ranked third of nine aspects of school that are supportive and enabling. As Dan explains, the use of a young person's interests to engage them in learning must extend beyond simply mentioning the topic of interest: *Yes that* [work based around interests] *would be better, but they can't just say '1 video game, plus 2 video games equals 3 video games'* (I/D/p5).

Timmy drew on his experiences in the AEP and indicated the benefit of a more flexible curriculum, and again not being forced: *Like here* [AEP], *if you don't like something you can replace it with something else.*

This extends to homework which, in itself, was one feature of the curriculum that acted as a barrier to enjoying mainstream education. Robert highlights the snowball effect when trying to keep up with the demands:

> It was kind of like a snowball going down a hill. So you go down the hill and you don't owe too much ... but as you go downhill further the work [snow] builds up further and further (I/Rob/p3).

Sarah-Jane notes how she struggled to record the homework task being given orally:

> I hated them [homeworks] (I/SJb/p4). I couldn't remember the homework ... in class she would have said the homework and someone would have talked to me and I would have forgotten it straight away [due to auditory processing difficulties] (I/SJb/p5).

Supportive environment

The physical and social environment within which the curricula, the pedagogy of teachers and pupils interact emerged as an area that, if adapted, can provide further support for the young people, albeit no common vision emerged. They identified having safe spaces to de-stress, more regular breaks, smaller class sizes, and the aesthetics of the school (and how this makes them feel).

Ro drew on their experiences of the study hub to describe what a supportive environment would be like. Predictability, her own routine (and not that imposed by the teacher or dictated by the curriculum of study), feeling safe with no fear of repercussions and flexibility are all important:

> It [study hub] is more relaxed. I know the people, the parents and all ... familiarity and relaxation helps. There is no real penalty for not getting something. There is more of a routine for me. I can sit down and do some work, have a break and get back into the work (I/Ro/p9). You know what to expect (I/Ro/p10).

Safe spaces to de-stress

Eleven participants specifically highlighted wanting a safe space to use to relax, de-stress and socialise with similar young people. Sarah-Jane, Dan, Wade, Thomas and Lee illustrate this:

> I think if they had have put something in place [a space to de-stress] I would have felt a little more comfortable (I/SJb/p1). It would be nice to have little areas in a classroom to escape to if stressed (I/SJb/p8).

> Yes it [a space] would help. Sometimes if I needed time alone ... it wouldn't be for every time I get upset but a small space would be for sometimes (I/D/p9).

> I would like my own safe space, but maybe not just for me on my own. I really wish there was something like that. The hub is the closest thing. Knowing it was there would have helped (I/W/p6).

> Time-out cards if really annoyed to go to chill out spaces. Comfortable places to hide in the classroom with headphones if stressed (MyIdSch/Th).

In the absence of a dedicated safe haven, Stephen found his own space to de-stress – the toilet:

> Sometimes I just went to the toilet to sit and breath in and out to try and relax and get away from all the noise and pressure (I/S/p2).

Robert highlighted that having such a space would need careful consideration due to the potential for it to be counterproductive:

> The problem would be that if other people went in there too then you would be nervous to go there. You know, if you were anxious and nervous and then had a room to go to but you didn't know who was there it would also make you nervous (I/Rob/p3).

Regular breaks

Similarly, six participants would like more breaks. Jim summarised why; to *get away from it all for a bit* (IdSch/Ji). He reflected on the AEP he attends where there is often flexibility for small breaks in and between classes. Jim explains: *breaks do help ... do this work and get five minutes on the computer* (I/Ji/p7).

Likewise, Dan spoke of the benefit of more frequent short breaks:

> I would like more frequent breaks – even if short. So I can imagine if I was going to school that even though I am going to do a lot of work, but overall I have some short and long breaks and see my friends, this would make me happy [joyous tone]! (I/D/p6).

Stephen explained why he needs more regular breaks, particularly with a trusted adult: *It is to offload any issues, calm down and get on with my work* (I/S/p6).

Having known Stephen for several school terms, the benefits of being able to offload rather than ruminate allowed him to release the stresses he experienced at home and school.

Smaller class sizes

They all want smaller class sizes to make mainstream education less overwhelming and more supportive and enabling. Some provided specific numbers of pupils, such as Dan and Sarah-Jane who suggested having five to ten pupils in a class, with Jim and Thomas both suggesting having two teachers within a class of five pupils. Wade also indicated this by suggesting his ideal school would have 50 staff and 100 pupils; all demonstrating the want for a higher staff-to-pupil ratio but within a school with a small overall pupil population.

Wade, Ro, Jim and Sarah-Jane, who also spoke of the negative impact of the noisy and busy mainstream school environment, explained that class sizes may afford teachers more time to offer support:

I think that is the problem with mainstream. There are too many children in the class. There is not time for the teacher to help me. They focus on one bad apple and when other children are having problems (I/W/p5).

Smaller classes and just time for teachers to be aware that certain students have certain difficulties with certain things and noticing that they have trouble with things and need support (I/Ro/p2). [Teachers] could notice more if a child is doing well or not and encourage them. Smaller schools would be more suitable for children with autism (I/Ro/p9).

There are too many people and the teachers don't have time for you, but here [AEP] there are less people and teachers can help and get to know you more (I/Ji/p9).

Rob drew upon their experiences of smaller classes in the AEP, where class sizes range from one-to-one to six young people:

Smaller classes really do help ... it helps make you feel more comfortable and able to be yourself (I/Rob/p7). In mainstream there would be 30 in one room but here [AEP] there are five in a room. This might be easier on the teacher. Here everything just feels more natural, it all flows better and easier and feels more natural and genuine (I/Rob/p5).

Ideal school

Participants used the 'My Ideal School' activity to give their thoughts on what the school environment would be like in order to best support them and reduce the stress they experience. Aside from thoughts already discussed – smaller class sizes and spaces to de-stress – participants such as Ro, Wade, Lee and Joe want lots of space to move around in, with large classrooms and fewer pupils to feel less trapped. Feeling safe is paramount. The ideal school for Robert and Lee would have lots of windows, particularly as their mainstream schools felt dark and oppressive. Joe would also like the corridor to have a glass ceiling so he could see out.

Jim and Joe described a very relaxed school, with sofas in the classroom. Jim calls this the 'school of identity', where people can be themselves.

Stephen also described his ideal school as being like a house – a place of safety – with his own individual work area. He drew the following picture (Figure 7.2).

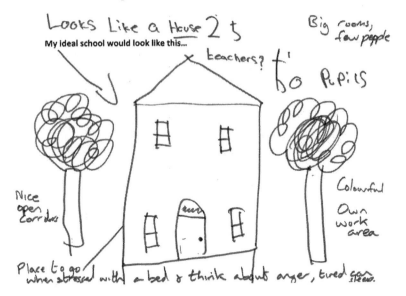

Figure 7.2 Stephen's ideal school

Several participants referred to the aesthetics of the classroom, although with no consensus. Sarah-Jane found navigating busy mainstream school corridors very stressful. To help alleviate this, her ideal school would have curved corridors. She explains why:

> Corridors that are more friendly – maybe curved. It would be great to take a few seconds and not make the corridors seem long and scary (MyIdSch/SJ).

Wade also noted the idea of safer-feeling curved corridors, his journey from class to class was fraught with bullying and social anxiety. His description of an ideal school – as illustrated below (Figure 7.3) – centred around the entire school environment being supportive and safe (inside and out):

> I feel it would be a one storey school ... it would be a big school but with only a few people. It would have one or two rooms for people to go to relax, you know to calm down if they need it. It would be curved inside to reduce the stress of seeing a full corridor of people. I like the idea of swirly corridors to keep out of the way when making my way down the corridor – places to sneak into for a few seconds. It would be perfect. Nature area at the front. Spaces

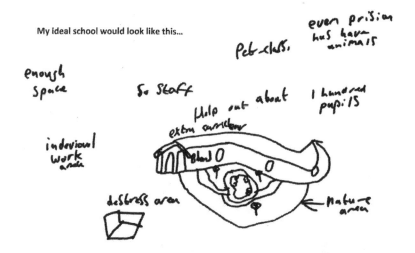

My ideal school would look like this...

even prision has have animals

Pet class.

enough space

So Staff

Help out about

extra cursclour

I hundred pupils

individual work area

destress area

new 0

nature area

Figure 7.3 Wade's ideal school

to de-stress outside if needed. Lots of space around the school. Individual work areas designed by pupils (MyIdSch/W).

He goes on to mention having a pet in school as *even prisoners have pets* (MyIdSch/W).

Similarly, Jack would like a pet in his ideal school: *To focus away from the stress* (MyIdSch/J).

Interestingly, Jack did not wish to draw an image of his ideal school (demonstrating the need for a flexible approach). Instead he wrote the word 'nothing' and, when asked, he elaborated by saying, *so autistic children wouldn't have to go to school* – reflecting the enormity of the negativity he feels about mainstream school. For Ro, the school ethos holds greater importance than physical features of the school environment. She explains:

It's not the building which matters, it's the attitude and atmosphere inside it ... as long as it is open, with quite a few rooms and lots of open spaces and lots of windows (MyIdSch/Ro).

Summary: how would autistic young people like school to be?

Participants explored several aspects of school they would like to change: teachers, curricula and the school environment. As with the literature, participants want teachers to be more understanding of them, of autism and of their individual needs (see Brede et al., 2017). They want teachers to adopt a flexible pedagogical approach and implement strategies carefully and not assume that a strategy should be used ubiquitously with every autistic young person. They also want teachers to be mindful of the implications of how they deliver the curriculum and of each child's circumstances. Above all, they want to be listened to – a characteristic highlighted when participants spoke of positive teachers that they have had.

They alluded to concepts of personhood and social justice. They want to be respected and valued as an individual person and not viewed as part of a homogeneous group because of the shared autistic label. They need the necessary, and not just equal, supports to be implemented to ensure they can not only access the curriculum but also be included in the learning and community of the classroom. Participants highlighted simple strategies, some of which are pertinent to one participant, while others suggested several. These include: breaking work and instructions down into more manageable chunks; supporting instructions visually; being able to use ICT more often to present work; having alternatives to auditory mental mathematics due to processing difficulties; using a child's interest to engage them (see Wood, 2019); being given time to socialise with peers; showing flexibility in the amount and content of homework; and providing homework in written form rather than relying on the young person having to block out the noise of others to write down the task that is being given orally.

Support can come from the school environment itself. As noted in the literature (such as Humphrey and Lewis, 2008b), participants want safe havens, or places to go to de-stress within school – to get away from it all – and to recalibrate and refocus. They also want more breaks for the same reasons. This aligns to literature that emphasises safe havens – or spaces to go – when feeling overwhelmed. However, any areas of support, such as 'quiet refuges' (Parsons et al., 2011, p.58) or 'safe havens' (Safran, 2002, p.62), must be positioned for easy access to negate the need to navigate complex and busy corridors.

Participants believe that smaller class sizes would improve mainstream education, allowing their teachers to support them more as they would have more time to give to each child. Smaller class sizes and a smaller pupil population (with a high staff-to-pupil ratio) would also reduce social anxiety and sensory overload. Several young people outlined that their ideal school would feel more relaxed and safe if classrooms were large, open spaces with sofas and, again, there were areas to take breaks and relax. This would help remove the feeling of being trapped.

For some, such as Ro, teacher mentality and school ethos were more important than aesthetics or location. The young people want something to strive for with teachers who have high expectations of their ability and without fear of repercussions for not knowing. As demonstrated in the literature, teachers hold a variety of attitudes to the inclusion of autistic young people in mainstream schools. These attitudes are influential in the process of inclusion (such as Glazzard, 2011; see Chapter Four).

How participants would like school to be mirrors some of the aspects to successful ASD inclusion outlined by Morewood, Humphrey and Symes (2011), who advocate a saturation model underpinned by staff training, peer awareness education, school environment modification, flexible provision and a positive ethos of autism acceptance and suitable policy.

8 Inclusion from the perspectives of autistic young people

Introduction

This chapter explores how autistic young people conceptualise inclusion; an area I found sparse within inclusion literature. First, I present how these young people describe autism. In previous chapters I highlighted the importance of how a disability such as autism is understood and the impact this can have on young people's part in research and their experiences in education – and, importantly, why it is vital to gain insight from autistic individuals themselves. For them, inclusion is a feeling (a sense of belonging), not a place (mainstream or otherwise).

What is autism?

The young people were asked 'what does autism mean to you?' This was followed by asking them how autism impacts on their time at school and how they feel about being autistic. As with the discussion on terminology earlier, those I asked preferred the term 'autistic child' over 'child with autism'. They offered a range of responses on what autism means to them.

For Ro, autism is a difference, like any other characteristic. This explains her preference for identity-first language (autistic child). She said, *If you are blond or brunette … it is something you live with and deal with. It is a difference.* She did mention having social skills difficulties.

Wade spoke of how he would exchange some intelligence in order to gain social skills. He spoke first of how autism makes him feel more intelligent, before focusing on deficits. He said, *it makes me feel more intelligent, but in my opinion part of my brain isn't working. I feel like there is something I can do more than what other children can do. Special isn't always better.*

Dan, Ro, Jim, Lee and Timmy referred to autism as a difference, or as them being different from others. Dan extended this by stating that *other people won't understand you ... it is hard.* Jim spoke of having social skills and of diversity within autism. He also views autism as a deficit: *It is something wrong with you. Like it's unique in a way. Everyone is different in their own way.*

Although preferring the term 'autistic child', Jack is negative about being autistic. He said, *autism is when your mind is changed. Very rarely a good thing.* Lee spoke only of negatives, relating to finding it difficult to concentrate when it is noisy. He, as did Stephen, spoke of autism causing him to get angry quickly. Timmy also, more cautiously however, spoke of autism being linked to being angry. He spoke of being autistic as an excuse he can use when playing games consoles or when he is in trouble. He stated:

> It is just a difference really. Sometimes people with autism don't like teachers and can get angry. I use it as an excuse when playing the 'games console' and to get away with things. 'Why are you doing that?' I have autism.

Lee and Thomas described how they were given a diagnosis, but without further information by professionals or parents about autism. Thomas said: *I am on the autistic spectrum, but I don't know what it means.* He attributed his ability to focus on areas of interest to being autistic.

Inclusion and Me

As we have heard, participants provided insider accounts of their individual educational journeys and how they could be better supported. These experiences underpin their thoughts on inclusion and, more specifically, their opinions on mainstream inclusion for autistic young people. Two activities focused specifically on inclusion. I sought their thoughts on the statement 'more children with autism are being made to go to mainstream school' and responses to the question 'What does school inclusion mean to you?'

In the 'beans and pots' activity, with reference to mainstream, only Robert chose 'true' to the statement 'I feel accepted in school', with only he and Stephen choosing 'true' to the statement 'I feel included in school'. The majority of the young people did not experience inclusion in mainstream. In other activities, participants highlighted key facets of inclusion, such as belonging, being accepted and feeling valued as a person – some of which were explored in Chapter Seven. Within this current chapter, and under the theme 'Inclusion and Me', two sub-themes will be expanded on: 'defining inclusion' and 'autism and mainstream inclusion'.

Defining inclusion

In the main, data pertaining to inclusion related to feelings associated with being included, the location or school type where inclusion takes place, what inclusion depends upon and, to a lesser extent, the participants' own personal experiences of being in mainstream school.

All participants are of the same opinion; inclusion can take place in any type of school. For them inclusion is not synonymous with mainstream. As Joe states: *Inclusion is being part of the school (any school), being happy and valued* (D/Jo). Ro furthers this by saying, *it is about the school mentality* (D/Ro).

Four participants – Stephen, Sarah-Jane, Ro and Jack – noted the difficulty they had with explaining inclusion. Sarah-Jane explains why:

> I find it difficult to understand the term 'inclusion', as my experience of education was that I was excluded and not included in a lot of ways such as making friends, socialising, in lessons etc. I was nearly always on my own and others would laugh at me if I didn't understand the work or got it wrong (D/SJ).

Sarah-Jane reflects on one of her experiences and describes the need for the necessary support to be in place for inclusion to be experienced in mainstream schools:

> [Inclusion] can be in any school. If the support isn't there in mainstream then it will never be inclusion … it can't be inclusion … you can't belong or be included if the help isn't there. It takes an awful lot of support and thought from the teacher to make sure children are included. Sometimes the wrong thing is done, such as saying 'get a partner …' often autistic children don't have anyone to go to so are left alone (D/SJ).

Similarly, Ro never felt included so she found it difficult to define the term. Nonetheless, she offered her thoughts on what inclusion is, or should be, who is involved in enabling inclusion and how it makes an included person feel:

I think some teachers think inclusion is just ask the pupils a question occasionally ... it's not that. It is more of a feeling of being happy, welcome and belonging in the environment (D/Ro).

The term 'belonging' was also noted by Wade and Jack, with Lee and Thomas using similar terms, such as 'being wanted' and 'having a place in the school'. Again, Stephen and Lee used the phrase 'being part of the group' to suggest belonging. Being valued was also mentioned by Joe, Stephen, Wade and Jack. Three participants described how being included is dependent on being recognised and respected for who they are as an individual – as a person. This mirrors thoughts discussed in Chapters Six and Seven with regard to feeling unsupported and being supported. Wade, Joe, Robert and Timmy explain:

It is more about how a person feels. Feeling valued as a person and feeling you matter (D/W).

It is when teachers and staff want to get to know you as a person and you feel you have a place there (D/Jo).

[Inclusion is] to be treated as a person not a figure (D/Ro).

It is about being respected as a person (D/Ti).

For Timmy, inclusion is founded upon teachers being mindful of his needs but, importantly, it is not about being forced to interact with peers if not wishing to do so: *Inclusion involves teachers being mindful of your needs, but not forcing you to be 'included' with other kids* (D/Ti).
Wade focused on the concept of fairness in his description of inclusion. He explains:

I think it should be fair for everyone. So if one child is struggling a wee bit they should get some help to make him feel happier ... this would be fair (D/W).

He illustrated this with a drawing of children trying to watch a game of football over a fence (Figure 8.1). For all to be included, fairly treated and have equal opportunity they don't just need the same support, but the necessary support – reflecting what Sarah-Jane mentioned above about inclusion being dependent on the support provided. Robert also notes: *Inclusion is to have the same chance as someone else* (D/Rob).

Figure 8.1 Wade illustrating fairness as integral to inclusion

Wade describes how inclusion is not a solitary experience, but involves others: *If included you are happy as you are with others, less lonely because you might feel included as there are others like you* (D/ W). Similarly for Jim, having friends underpins inclusion: *It is being involved, having friends, talking and doing work with people* (D/Ji).

Autism and mainstream inclusion

Participants discussed their thoughts on mainstream inclusion, the barriers that exist to inclusion and what would help support autistic young people in mainstream (some are presented in Goodall, 2018a). Some were negative in response to 'more children with autism are being made to go to mainstream school', suggesting this is a bad idea. Others offered more pragmatic thoughts emphasising the complex interaction between each individual's characteristics, autism and mainstream. However, crucially, no participant thought mainstream for all was a good idea.

Robert provides an analogy to illustrate his thoughts on how, for him, inclusion for all young people in one school is not fair, nor possible:

> I believe this isn't right, as the child might not be able to cope. It is just like an ingredient … like a big pot … you can't just throw every ingredient in … only certain ingredients work with other ingredients (D/Rob).

Similarly, Wade stated that autism and mainstream do not really go together. He drew a 'toxic monster' to represent that mainstream for all autistic children is a bad idea, but also to reflect his experiences and description of mainstream as a toxic environment (Figure 8.2).

Jack also stated that making more children with autism go to mainstream school is a bad idea and drew a sad and angry character to represent his thoughts (Figure 8.3).

Dan expressed his frustration with mainstream – in particular the teachers. He represented his thoughts about the statement by drawing a teacher being hit with knives (Figure 8.4). He said the idea is *Evil. Teachers don't really care. 'Teacher', to me, is just like evil* (C/D). Importantly, with regard to participating in decisions, Dan – as do Robert and Jim – also wants autistic young people to have the choice in whether or not they go to mainstream school.

Timmy suggests that the potential success of a mainstream placement depends on the severity of the individual's autism. He represented this by drawing a face that is both smiling and sad (Figure 8.5). He

Figure 8.2 Wade's toxic monster

Figure 8.3 Jack's sad and angry character

Figure 8.4 Dan's drawing of a teacher being hit by knives

Figure 8.5 Timmy's happy and sad illustration

goes on to state that: *It's not fair to make children go to mainstream school if they can't cope or it doesn't support them* (C/Ti).

I wanted to gauge opinion on having the choice of attending a school solely for autistic children as an alternative to mainstream. The statement 'I would attend a school for only children with ASD' was included in the 'beans and pots' activity. The young people offered an equal spread of responses across 'true', 'not sure' and 'untrue' to this statement.

Ro expanded on her 'unsure' response by stating, *wherever is best – as long as it is autism friendly.* This is consistent with her views on inclusion, her own struggles with mainstream school and thoughts on her ideal school; that the mentality within the school and of the teachers is fundamentally important, and that the necessary support must be in place for inclusion to truly happen and be felt. For Ro, inclusion does not rely on a particular type of school.

For Wade, the idea of a school for autistic children is a positive alternative to mainstream. There would be commonality with peers – that sense of belonging. He explains: *You would be around other children who would be going through the same thing as you* (C/W).

Sarah-Jane explains that placing all children with autism in mainstream is not a good idea. She elaborated and referred to her experiences of bullying, peer ignorance about autism and the lack of teacher support experienced in mainstream:

> Many pupils in mainstream schools don't understand anything about autism. I think it would leave the person with autism open to bullying from peers and be thought of as some kind of weirdo by the other pupils. Finding friends and maintaining friendships might prove difficult, leaving the person with autism alone and isolated. The idea of someone with autism attending a mainstream school is great if the support is in place. This may involve adapting the curriculum as well as changing how a subject is taught. Teaching staff might have to readjust their thinking and attitudes towards someone with autism and how they can best provide support. Not a good idea [for all] because people have different learning techniques and how they learn is different (C/SJ).

Stephen also notes the risk of bullying: *This is a bad idea because of bullies. People call you names like 'retard', 'special bastard' and 'spastic'* (C/S).

Joe also reflected on his own educational experiences of exclusion from mainstream:

> It is a bad thing – like me, they will get thrown out because the schools aren't able to give the support of help with their needs or challenging behaviour. Teachers need more training, understanding and fewer children to deal with (C/Jo).

Stephen, Lee and Jim do not believe all autistic children should be made to attend a mainstream school, premised on the lack of support available:

There isn't enough support from teachers to help autistic kids. Teachers need to be understanding and help (C/S).

No [children with autism shouldn't be made to go to mainstream school], they need more help and you don't get that in mainstream. Teachers don't really know what to do in mainstream (C/L).

Teachers are not trained enough or don't understand (C/Ji).

Wade suggests that, without support, attending mainstream school is even worse:

Mainstream schools don't support people with disabilities as I found out from my experiences. Mmm ... there just isn't the support ... being forced to go then this is even worse (C/W).

Ro echoed these thoughts. For mainstream inclusion to work, autistic young people need to be:

Understood and listened too and rather than them [teachers] just patronising you and telling you to go and sit on your own until you are okay. For me it is just a matter of knowing if your students have problems or not (C/Ro).

Figure 8.6 Ro's indifferent face

Figure 8.7 Illustration of mainstream versus a suitable school for autistic kids

Ro drew an indifferent face (Figure 8.6), but also suggests the face shows concern and worry about more children with autism being made to go to mainstream schools.

For Stephen, Jim and Thomas the challenges posed by the large school population and sensory environment of mainstream – as noted in Chapter Six – are a barrier to mainstream inclusion for autistic young people:

> There are just too many people – it is too noisy, busy and stressful for children with autism. If more children with autism go to mainstream there would be more fights as the children couldn't cope (C/S).

Jim states: [There are] *too many people in a big mainstream school* (C/Ji).

Thomas illustrates his thoughts with a drawing of two schools (Figure 8.7). The mainstream school is shrouded in clouds and the other – a suitable school for autistic kids – is underneath a bright rainbow.

Summary: what does school inclusion mean to autistic young people; how do they define and describe inclusion?

The above discussion and the perspectives of the young people therein demonstrate that inclusion in mainstream is not suitable, nor necessarily possible, for all autistic children. There are many changeable variables that create the mismatch between the mainstream school environment and the needs of autistic learners. Participants noted several barriers to inclusion in mainstream, such as that teachers do not understand autism, teachers do not have the necessary knowledge of autism or want to support autistic young people, the challenges posed by the sensory environment (particularly in larger secondary schools) and large class sizes limiting the amount of time a teacher can afford to young people who need it.

In line with the literature, no single definition of inclusion emerged from the young people – some, such as Ro and Sarah-Jane, found it difficult to describe inclusion as they never felt included. There were, however, recurring responses that centred on the feelings and principles associated with inclusion, such as happiness, support and understanding from teachers and their peers, feeling secure to be themselves by being valued as an individual, respected for who they are and feeling that they belong, as opposed to being the unnoticed outsider.

Acceptance and belonging are connected concepts and feelings which impact greatly upon each other. Crouch, Keys and McMahon (2014) suggest that children with SEND feel accepted when they experience positive interactions with others. Where they consider themselves respected, valued and treated fairly in line with their peers there is greater likelihood they will then feel accepted as part of a group and belonging within the same environment as others. Baumeister and Leary (1995) described belonging as a fundamental human need which supports the individual to feel motivated to be part of a community, such as a school. The creation of an environment in which children feel accepted and the development of a sense of belonging in whichever school context they are in are critical to inclusion.

It is apparent that the participants do not equate the term inclusion with mainstream school. Inclusion, for them, is not dependent on location. Being in a mainstream school does not automatically grant inclusion. For them inclusion can be found in any type of school, so long as the support is in place. And, for some, inclusion could have been a reality if they had been afforded a choice of where to be educated, such as alternative education (see Goodall, 2019). But, again, they reflected on the need to consider each individual's needs and characteristics. To pursue full inclusion – the right to inclusive education, as proclaimed by the UNCRPD – could be considered at 'all costs', and may oppose what is actually in the child's best interests or, indeed, what they want.

Participants discussed their thoughts on the momentum for more autistic young people being educated in mainstream school, the barriers that exist to inclusion and what would help support autistic young people in mainstream. They oppose the concept of universal inclusion. They do, however, align to the premise of moderate inclusion, in that some participants suggested mainstream can work for some autistic young people when the necessary support is in place. Support extends beyond strategies to include the school ethos and teacher mentality being such that every young person is listened to and teachers want to help in an understanding and flexible manner.

The relational pedagogical aspects of their education, such as the interactions and relationships their teachers built with them, underpinned the extent to which they felt they belonged, wanted and, ultimately, included. Young people spoke of specific teachers with whom they had positive experiences. These teachers were non-judgemental, personable, caring, accepting and understanding. Importantly, these teachers, albeit few in number, adhered to the Inclusive Pedagogical Approach discussed in Chapter Two; they were non-deterministic, flexible in their approach and accepted the young person's 'difference'.

9   Conclusion

At the beginning of this book I presented theoretical and rights perspectives on educational inclusion (Chapters Two and Three). I then outlined the fractured nature of educational inclusion for autistic young people (Chapter Four), the challenges posed by the mainstream environment and the potential negative impacts this can have on the young person. Our understanding of inclusion for autistic learners remains limited because the research is overwhelmingly reported from adult perspectives; learners' voices are sparse in the literature. In Chapter Five I detailed practical and theoretical considerations for developing rights-based inclusive participatory research to ensure that these voices are heard in an authentic autism-considered framework. I then presented the narratives of 12 autistic young people (Chapters Six to Eight). They discussed their educational experiences, their thoughts on school improvement and how they conceptualise, describe and experience inclusion, thereby demonstrating how we – as allies of autistic children and young people – can be better informed to better support them through meaningful research.

> They have shown that their educational challenges are compounded by environmental and attitudinal barriers which the schools have failed to remove. These young people showed that they are experts in their own lives, of their autism, and should be given the space to disseminate their experiences to enable more autism self-advocacy, as Woods (2017) highlights. They must be central to the educational change and improvement to make school more suitable and inclusive. (Goodall, 2018b, p.3)

My research supported autistic young people to share their narratives in a manner that respected their rights, recognising them as beings with capacity, with 'much to share'. The participants and the research advisory group before them were supported in having their voices heard in a non-tokenistic and meaningful way. The study, and this book as a whole, provides a valuable perspective and deep insight into the educational experiences of this under-represented group in the literature. The young people we heard from shared many and varied educational experiences – some positive, but mainly negative – and reflected on aspects of education which hinder and support access to and enjoyment in education. For them, attempts at inclusion in mainstream resulted in exclusion and, for some, impacted on their wellbeing.

Where are we now?

A chasm exists between research, policy and practice – although in many regards this gap is narrowing, with more emphasis being placed on hearing the voices of autistic young people themselves (especially autistic females). However, mainstream 'inclusion for all' is still an agenda at the forefront of education systems across the developed world, with a scarcity of research exploring how young people who find mainstream most challenging feel about this.

There is no doubt that mainstream school is beneficial for many. Many schools are providing appropriate support for SEND pupils and these schools should be recognised and applauded for their inclusivity and not penalised during inspection processes seeking hard outcome data (as discussed earlier in this book). However, the research I undertook demonstrates that mainstream inclusion for all is not working, as autistic young people can become educational collateral damage, who then, if they are fortunate enough, find a place of belonging elsewhere, such as in the Alternative Education Provision (AEP) where I teach. Many are already switched off from education by then.

Undoubtedly there is scope for change (see Goodall, 2015a). However, even the most recent policy frameworks, such as those here in Northern Ireland (Chapter Two), advocate for inclusion yet often appear wedded to medicalised 'individual-as-deficit' concepts of disability. Inclusion in mainstream may become a reality for more autistic young people when their expert voices are heard through participatory, inclusive and non-tokenistic ways in research. But, and it is an enormous 'but' that cannot be swept aside, the complex interplay of multiple variables (geographical, sensory, attitudinal, social, pedagogical and biological to name a few) means that mainstream school and teachers cannot ensure that all these young people are supported as they should be, thus impacting on, and changing how, they access, experience and succeed in education. Influencing teacher attitudes so that they understand autism and accept autistic people in their classes is one step, and, by being accepted, fewer children will have to camouflage or mask who they are. If our education system continues to focus on examination outcomes – the hard data – then it is difficult to conceive a time when change can happen quickly enough, if at all.

Teachers' attitudes in the classroom and their teaching approaches are essentially underpinned by philosophical beliefs. These beliefs could relate to the teachers' role within the classroom, their views on the purpose of education, or their opinions regarding educational agendas, such as the drive for the inclusion of pupils with a wider range of needs in mainstream schools. From professional experience I have found that, for pupils who have been excluded – formally or informally – from mainstream education, the attitudes held by teachers underpin how engaged they are, or are likely to be, with the educational process. It proves difficult to rebuild the value of education for many of them. Pupils I work with often express experiences of negative attitudes held by previous teachers; many of these pupils could not cope with main-stream school and opted out through non-attendance. Engaging autistic young people in participatory research and gaining greater under-standing of how they experience education and want to be supported will hopefully, eventually, enact positive change. By authentically researching with them we are advocating for their voices to be heard.

In light of the experiences of the young people in this book, inclusion, as a process and an agenda, should be conceived more broadly, shifting the definition beyond the confines of mainstream schools – separating the interchanging terms of 'mainstream' and 'inclusion' to a feeling and experience that can be located in any type of school. In the literature review I discussed how adults debated the concept of inclusion as one mainly relating to theoretical positions on the extent to or level at which inclusion should take place, and the educational structures within which it is dependent, namely mainstream settings. However, the perspectives of the young people in this study challenge notions of inclusion by the-orising, conceptualising and defining it somewhat differently – albeit while not arriving at a singular definition. Inclusion, for these young people, is conceived beyond the universal-moderate inclusionist debate and is not confined to mainstream school. As discussed, it is a feeling of belonging. In short, they want to be understood, respected, supported, valued and included. Difficulties with mainstream inclusion for these young people arise from the interaction between factors within the school environment, including teacher understanding, teacher knowl-edge, peer ignorance and sensory, social and geographical aspects of the school environment. Inclusion in mainstream schools, as I discussed in Chapter Three, is considered a right. However, this study demonstrates that a needs-based argument is also important in ensuring access to suitable education that furthers the rights of each young person.

As I stated in Goodall (2018b, p.1663):

> The lives and experiences of these children – the reality of 'inclusion' – should be our guide to improving education, not ideology. It is not acceptable to continue the pursuit of full inclusion without considering the impact on those children who might become, arguably, educational collateral damage. They matter too. We should be mindful that schools are to serve children, not adults (as expressed by Warnock, 2005).

For them, inclusion is defined as belonging, being valued, of social justice and, importantly, should be uncoupled from the term 'mainstream'. The young people have provided insight into why individual difference is important for supporting need and respecting a person's individuality – Jim expressed this when drawing his ideal school, calling it the 'school of identity'. Inclusion is being able to be oneself by being respected, valued and accepted by teachers and peers for the person who they are. It is about having relationships with others, being happy, safe and being part of the school community rather than being the outsider looking in.

The young people do not feel that all autistic children can experience inclusion in mainstream settings, opposing the concept of universal mainstream inclusion. Instead, the stance of moderate inclusion is supported by the young people in this study. In the main, the young people recognise that mainstream education should be the goal when appropriate and when the necessary support is in place, but that this should not be forced. This supports the Committee on the Rights of Persons with Disabilities General Comment 4 (United Nations, 2016), which states that without accompanying structural changes to create an accessible built environment, such as modifying teaching methods and approaches, placing a child with disabilities in a mainstream classroom does not constitute inclusion. Cognisance of the views of autistic young people, such as those we have heard, would go a long way to fulfilling the vision of Article 24 of the UNCRPD, to develop 'human potential, sense of dignity and self worth'; and the strengthening of respect for human rights, fundamental freedoms and diversity in our educational establishments.

The young people offered advice on how education for them and other autistic young people could be improved to make it more enjoyable, supportive and enabling. The characteristics of a supportive (or good) teacher have been explored. Their thoughts echo that of Temple Grandin (1996) – an autistic woman – who said 'some teachers just have a knack for working with autistic children. Other teachers do not have it'; and, as Chapters Six to Eight demonstrated, the person the teacher is, their ability to show genuine interest in the individual, is of utmost importance to these young people. Relational aspects, the connections, teachers' ability to engender trust, safety, happiness and positive expectation are cornerstones of education (inclusion and research). It goes beyond having training or implementing specific strategies, to showing a genuine interest in a pupil as a person. However, that is not to say flexible, tailored educational approaches are not considered crucial (see Martin et al., 2019) – they are, and this has been reflected by the young people in this book when discussing school improvement (see Chapter Eight).

With a participatory rights-based approach, which enables researcher-participant relationships to be developed, the young people you have heard from demonstrate that autistic young people can – and should – contribute to the discussion on their educational provision. They are the experts on their lives, and without their individual perspectives educators and policymakers will always remain as outsiders looking in trying to judge what is best. In a way, this book is a 'call to arms' to understand the educational experiences and voices of autistic young people.

Personal reflection

I have taught for 12 years in an AEP where many children, some autistic, arrive disaffected, switched off and anxious about education because of their previous experiences. Some have been absent from school for several months and lack confidence or motivation to re-engage with education. Those who do engage state that teacher understanding, acceptance and flexibility are core enablers of inclusion, allowing them to feel supported, valued, accepted and understood. Conducting the research presented here has let me explore the educational experiences of 12 very different young people and contribute to the limited body of knowledge on autistic young people's educational experiences and thoughts on inclusion. The study – as qualitative research does – explains and rediscovers what has happened, why, and searches for truth. It has also shown me that supporting autistic young people is more complex than simply implementing a variety of ASD strategies. Whether research or education, it is about relationships. And it is about treating each child as an individual and understanding and truly respecting them for the person they are.

As a practitioner-researcher working daily with autistic young people I was well aware of the complexities of the lives of autistic young people. The (not insurmountable) challenges outlined in Chapter Five, in part, help to explain why there remains a dearth of research with autistic young people (and others at risk of educational exclusion). However, there ought not to be. These voices are needed to better understand the efficacy of mainstream inclusion for autistic young people and I hope this book inspires more research in this area. Lots of flexibility and understanding is required, and then some. Working with these young people in the study has also proven beneficial to me, affirming my ability as an educator to build trusting relationships with young people. I am privileged that the young people trusted me to support them in exercising their rights and sharing their experiences and perspectives. I am still humbled by this. Several young people spoke of how they enjoyed participating in the research, with Dan and Ro noting that they felt their experiences were finally being listened to and validated.

The right to inclusive education was outlined in Chapter Three, but from the experiences of many of the participants one asks: is a traditional 'mainstream school' approach the correct mode of education for *all* autistic children and young people? Personally, in light of the testimonies of those who participated in my study, the literature and my years of experience, I am more convinced that this is not the case. This research has not only affirmed for me the importance of understanding each and every young person as an individual, but has also persuaded me that my thoughts on inclusion – as a moderate inclusionist – are needed and should underpin policy and practice to better support autistic young people. For the young people in this study, inclusion is a feeling, a sense of belonging, and not a place, mainstream or otherwise.

References

Ainscow, M. (2014) From special education to effective schools for all: Widening the agenda (pp.171–186). In Florian, L. (Ed.) *The SAGE handbook of special education* (2nd edition), Volume 1. London: Sage.

Aluwihare-Samaranayake, D. (2015) Ethics in qualitative research: A view of the participants' and researchers' world from a critical standpoint. *International Journal of Qualitative Methods*, 11(2): 64–81.

Ambler, P.G., Eidels, A.and Gregory, C. (2015) Anxiety and aggression in adolescents with autism spectrum disorders attending mainstream schools. *Research in Autism Spectrum Disorders*, 18, 97–109.

Archard, D. (2004) *Children, rights and childhood* (2nd edition). London: Routledge.

Arnstein, S.R. (1969) A ladder of citizen participation. *Journal of the American Planning Association*, 35(4): 216–224.

Arthur-Kelly, M., Sutherland, D., Lyons, G., MacFarlane, S. and Foreman, P. (2013) Reflections on enhancing pre-service teacher education programmes to support inclusion: Perspective from New Zealand and Australia. *European Journal of Special Needs Education*, 28: 217–233.

Artiles, A.J., Kozleski, E.B., Dorn, S. and Christensen, C. (2006) Chapter 3: learning in inclusive education research: re-mediating theory and methods with transformative agenda. *Review of Research in Education*, 30: 65–108.

Attwood, T. (2007) *The complete guide to Asperger's Syndrome*. London: Jessica Kingsley Publishers.

Autism Act Northern Ireland (2011) http://www.legislation.gov.uk/nia/2011/27/contents/enacted (last accessed 15th May 2019).

Autistica (2016) *Personal tragedies, public crisis: The urgent need for a national response to early death in autism*. London: Autistica.

Bagnoli, A. (2009) Beyond the standard interview: the use of graphic elicitation and arts-based methods. *Qualitative Research*, 9(5): 547–570.

Baker, D.L. (2011) *The politics of neurodiversity: Why public policy matters*. Boulder, CO: Lynne Rienner.

Bainham, A. and Gilmore, S. (2013) *Children: The modern law* (4th edition). Bristol, UK: Jordan Publishing Limited.

Baldwin, S. and Costley, D. (2016) The experiences and needs of female adults with high-functioning autism spectrum disorder. *Autism*, 20(4): 483–495.

Barnes, C. (2012) Understanding the social model of disability: Past, present and future (pp.12–29). In Watson, N.Roulstone, A. and Thomas, C. (Eds.) *The Routledge handbook of disability studies*. London: Routledge.

Barton, L. (Ed.) (1998) *The politics of special educational needs*. Lewes, UK: Falmer.

Baumeister, R.F. and Leary, M.R. (1995) The need to belong: Desire for interpersonal attachments as a fundamental human motivation. *Psychological Bulletin*, 117: 497–529.

BBC (2018) Homeschooling in the UK increases 40% over three years. https://www.bbc.co.uk/news/uk-england-42624220 (last accessed 7th March 2019).

Bernier, R. and Gerdts, J. (2010) *Autism spectrum disorders: A reference handbook*. Santa Barbara, CA: ABC-CLIO.

Bettleheim, B. (1967) *The empty fortress: infantile autism and the Birth of the Self*. Oxford, UK: Free Press of Glencoe.

Bond, C. and Hebron, J. (2015) Developing mainstream provision for pupils with autism spectrum disorder: staff perceptions and satisfaction. *European Journal of Special Needs Education*, 31(2): 250–263.

Boujut, E., Popa-Roch, M., Palomares, E.M., Dean, A. and Cappe, E. (2017) Self-efficacy and burnout in teachers of students with autism spectrum disorder. *Research in Autism Spectrum Disorders*, 36: 8–20.

Boylan, J. and Dalrymple, J. (2009) *Understanding advocacy for children and young people*. Maidenhead, UK: McGraw-Hill International.

Braun, V. and Clarke, V. (2006) Using thematic analysis in psychology. *Qualitative Research in Psychology*, 3(2): 77–101.

Braun, V. and Clarke, V. (2014) *Successful qualitative research: a practical guide for beginners*. London: Sage Publications.

Brede, J., Remington, A., Kenny, L., Warren, K. and Pellicano, E. (2017) Excluded from school: Autistic students' experiences of school exclusion and subsequent re-integration into school. *Autism and Developmental Language Impairments*, 2: 1–20.

Brown, B.T., Morris, G., Nida, R.E. and Baker-Ward, L. (2012) Brief report: making experience personal: internal state language in the memory narratives of children with and without Asperger's disorder. *Journal of Autism and Developmental Disorders*, 42: 441–446.

Bryman, A. (2012) *Social research methods* (4th edition). Oxford, UK: Oxford University Press.

Byrne, B. (2012) Chapter 24: Minding the gap? Children with disabilities and the United Nations convention on the rights of persons with disabilities (pp. 419–437). In Freeman, M. (Ed.) *Law and childhood studies, current legal issues*, Volume 14. Oxford, UK: Oxford University Press.

Byrne, B. (2013) Hidden contradictions and conditionality: Conceptualisations of inclusive education in international law. *Disability and Society*, 28(2): 232–244.

Byrne, B. (2019) Article 23: children with disabilities. In Tobin, J. (Ed.) *The UN convention on the rights of the child: A commentary (Oxford commentaries on international law)*. Oxford, UK: Oxford University Press.

Cage, E. and Troxell-Whitman, Z. (2019) Understanding the reasons, contexts and costs of camouflaging for autistic adults. *Journal of Autism and Developmental Disorders*, 49: 1899–1911.

Carpenter, B., Happé, F. and Egerton, J. (2019) *Girls and autism: educational, family and personal perspectives*. Oxford, UK: Routledge.

Cassidy, S., Bradley, P., Robinson, J., Allison, C., McHugh, M. and Baron-Cohen, S. (2014) Suicidal ideation and suicide plans or attempts in adults with Asperger's Syndrome attending a specialist diagnostic clinic: a clinical cohort study. *Lancet Psychiatry*, 1: 142–147.

Centre for Studies in Inclusive Education (2004) Reasons against segregated schooling. http://inclusion.uwe.ac.uk/csie/reasonsagstsegschooling.pdf (last accessed 17th December 2015).

Chamberlain, B., Kasari, C. and Rotheram-Fuller, E. (2007) Involvement or isolation? The social networks of children with autism in regular classrooms. *Journal of Autism and Developmental Disorders*, 37: 230–242.

Chaney, P. (2012) Additional learning needs policy in the devolved polities of the UK: a systems perspective. *Journal of Research on Special Educational Needs*, 12: 28–36.

Children and Families Act (2014) London: The Stationery Office.

Cigman, R. (2007) A question of universality: inclusive education and the principle of respect. *Journal of Philosophy of Education*, 41(4): 775–793.

Cigman, R. (2010) Inclusion (pp. 158–163). In Peterson, P., Baker, E. and McGaw, B. (Eds.) *International encyclopaedia of education* (3rd edition). Kidlington, UK: Elsevier.

Clark, J. (2012) Using diamond ranking as visual cues to engage young people in the research process. *Qualitative Research Journal*, 12(2): 222–237.

Clark, A. and Moss, P. (2001) *Listening to young children: The mosaic approach*. London: National Children's Bureau.

Cleary, A. and Hayes, G. (2012) An exploration of Irish teachers' perceptions of the inclusion of children with Autistic spectrum disorders in mainstream primary schools (pp. 85–102). In Day, T. and Travers, J. (Eds.) (2012) *Special and inclusive education: A research perspective*. Bern: Peter Lang AG.

Cohen, L., Manion, L. and Morrison, K. (2011) *Research methods in education* (7th edition). London: Routledge.

Coleman-Fountain, E. (2017) Uneasy encounters: Youth, social (dis)comfort and the autistic self. *Social Science and Medicine*, 185: 9–16.

Conn, C. (2014) *Autism and the social model of childhood: A sociocultural perspective on theory and practice*. Oxford, UK: Routledge.

Conn, C. (2015) Essential conditions for research with children with autism: Issues raised by two case studies. *Children and Society*, 29: 59–68.

Connor, M. (2000) Asperger Syndrome (ASD) and the self-reports of comprehensive school students. *Educational Psychology in Practice*, 16: 285–296.

Cook-Sather, A. (2002) Authorising students' perspectives: toward trust, dialogue, and change in education. *Educational Researcher,* 31(3): 3–14.

Cook-Sather, A. (2006) Sound, presence and power: Exploring "student voice" in educational research and reform. *Curriculum Inquiry,* 36(4): 359–390.

Cook-Sather, A. (2007) Resisting the impositional potential of student voice work: lessons for liberatory educational research from poststructuralist feminist critiques of critical pedagogy. *Discourse: Studies in the Cultural Politics of Education,* 28(3): 389–403.

Cooper, K., Smith, L.G.E. and Russel, A.J. (2018) Gender identity in autism: Sex differences in social affiliation with gender groups. *Journal of Autism and Developmental Disorders,* 48(12): 3995–4006.

Crane, L., Adams, F., Harper, G., Welch, J. and Pellicano, E. (2019) 'Something needs to change': Mental health experiences of young autistic adults in England. *Autism,* 23(2): 477–493.

Cremin, H., Mason, C. and Busher, H. (2011) Problematising pupil voice using visual methods: findings from a study of engaged and disaffected pupils in urban secondary school. *British Educational Research Journal,* 37(4): 585–603.

Crouch, R., Keys, C.B. and McMahon, S.D. (2014) Student–teacher relationships matter for school inclusion: School belonging, disability, and school transitions. *Journal of Prevention and Intervention in the Community,* 42(1): 20–30.

Davies, M.B. (2007) *Doing a successful research project: using qualitative or quantitative methods.* Basingstoke, UK: Palgrave Macmillan.

De Beco, G. (2014) The right to inclusive education according to Article 24 of the UN convention on the rights of persons with disabilities: Background, requirements and (remaining) questions. *Netherlands Quarterly of Humans Rights,* 32(3): 263–287.

De Beco, G. (2016) Transition to inclusive education systems according to the convention on the rights of persons with disabilities. *Nordic Journal of Human Rights,* 34(1): 40–59.

Denzin, N.K. and Lincoln, Y.S. (2011) *The SAGE handbook of qualitative research* (4th edition). Los Angeles; London: Sage.

Department for Education (2009) *Every school a good school: The way forward for special educational needs and inclusion.* Bangor, UK: DoE.

Department for Education (2012) *Exclusion from maintained schools, academies and pupil referral units in England: A guide for those with legal responsibilities in relation to exclusion.* London: DoE.

Department for Education (England) (2015) *Special educational needs in England: January 2015.* https://www.gov.uk/government/statistics/special-educational-needs-in-england-january-2015 (last accessed 27th April 2016).

Department for Education (2017) Circular 2017/12 update on the new SEN framework. Bangor; Northern Ireland: DoE.

Department for Education (2018) Investigative research into alternative provision. London: DoE.

Department of Education (Northern Ireland) (1998) Code of practice on the identification and assessment of special educational needs. Bangor, UK: DENI.

Department of Education (Northern Ireland) (2002) Report of the task group on autism. Bangor, UK: DENI.

Department of Education (Northern Ireland) (2005) The special educational needs and disability (Northern Ireland) order. Bangor, UK: DENI.

Department of Health, Social Services and Public Safety (DHSSPSNI) (2019) The prevalence of autism (including Asperger's Syndrome) in school age children in Northern Ireland 2019. DHSSPSNI.

De Valenzuela, J.S. (2014) Sociocultural views of learning (pp. 299–314). In Florian, L. (Ed.) *The SAGE handbook of special education* (2nd edition), Volume 1. London: Sage.

Dockett, S. and Perry, B. (2005) Researching with children: insights from the Starting School Research Project. *Early Child Development and Care*, 175 (6): 507–521.

Driessnack, M. (2006) Draw-and-tell conversations with children about fear. *Qualitative Health Research*, 16(10): 1414–1435.

Eekelaar, J. (1986) The emergence of children's rights. *Oxford Journal of Legal Studies*, 6(2): 161–182.

Eekelaar, J. (1992) The importance of thinking that children have rights. *International Journal of Law, Policy and the Family*, 6: 221–235.

Eekelaar, J. (2007) *Family law and personal life.* Oxford, UK: Oxford University Press.

Ekins, A. (2015) *The changing face of special educational needs.* London: Routledge.

Eldar, E., Talmor, R. and Wolf-Zukerman, T. (2010) Success and difficulties in the individual inclusion of children with Autism Spectrum Disorder (ASD) in the eyes of their coordinators. *International Journal of Inclusive Education*, 14(1): 97–114.

Ellis, J. (2017) Researching the social worlds of autistic children: An exploration of how an understanding of autistic children's social worlds is best achieved. *Children and Society*, 31(1): 23–36.

Emam, M.M. and Farrell, P. (2009) Tensions experienced by teachers and their views of support for pupils with autism spectrum disorders in mainstream schools. *European Journal of Special Needs Education*, 24(4): 407–422.

Equality Commission for Northern Ireland (2008) *Every child an equal child.* Belfast: Equality Commission for Northern Ireland.

Eslea, M., Menesini, E., Morita, Y., O'Moore, M., Mora-Merchan, J.A., Periera, B., Smith, P.K. and Zhang, W. (2004) Friendship and loneliness among bullies and victims: Data from seven countries. *Aggressive Behaviour*, 30(1): 71–83.

European Convention on Human Rights (1950) (Revised 1996) Strasbourg: Council of Europe.

Evans, J. and Lunt, I. (2002) Inclusive education: Are there limits? *European Journal of Special Needs Education*, 17(1): 1–14.

Fayette, R. and Bond, C. (2018) A systematic literature review of qualitative research methods for eliciting the views of young people with ASD about their educational experiences. *European Journal of Special Needs Education*, 33(3): 349–365.

Federle, K.H. (1994) Rights flow downhill. *International Journal of Children's Rights*, 2(4): 343–368.

Federle, K.H. (2009) Review essay: Rights, not wrongs. *International Journal of Children's Rights*, 17: 321–329.

Fletcher-Watson, S. and Happé, F. (2019) *Autism: A new introduction to psychological theory and current debate*. Oxford and New York: Routledge.

Fletcher-Watson, S., Adams, J., Brook, K., Charman, T., Crane, L., Cusack, J., Leekam, S., Milton, D., Parr, J.R. and Pellicano, E. (2019) Making the future together: Shaping autism research through meaningful participation. *Autism*, 23(4): 943–953.

Florian, L. (2014a) Reimagining special education: Why new approaches are needed. In Florian, L. (Ed.) *The SAGE handbook of special education* (2nd edition), Volume 1. London: Sage.

Florian, L. (2014b) Inclusive pedagogy: An alternative approach to difference and inclusion (pp. 218–229). In Kiuppis, F. and Hausstatter, R.J. (Eds.) *Inclusive education twenty years after Salamanca*. New York: Peter Lang Publishing.

Florian, L. and Rouse, M. (2001) Inclusive practices in English secondary schools: Lessons learned. *Cambridge Journal of Education*, 31(3): 399–412.

Folstein, S. and Rutter, M. (1977) Infantile autism: A genetic study of 21 twin pairs. *Journal of Child Psychology and Psychiatry*, 18(4): 297–321.

Fortin, J. (2009) *Children's rights: The developing law* (3rd edition). Cambridge, UK: Cambridge University Press.

Frederickson, N., Jones, A.P. and Lang, J. (2010) Inclusive provision options for pupils on the autistic spectrum. *Journal of Research in Special Educational Needs*, 10(2): 63–73.

Freeman, M. (2000) The future of children's rights. *Children and Society*, 14: 277–293.

Freeman, M. (Ed.) (2012) *Law and childhood studies: current issues 2011*, Volume 14. Oxford University Press.

Gernsbacher, M.A. (2017) Editorial perspective: The use of person-first language in scholarly writing may accentuate stigma. *Journal of Child Psychology and Psychiatry*, 58: 859–861.

Gibb, K., Tunbridge, D., Chua, A. and Frederickson, N. (2007) Pathways to inclusion: Moving from special school to mainstream. *Educational Psychology in Practice*, 23(2): 109–127.

Glazzard, J. (2011) Perceptions of the barriers to effective inclusion in one primary school: Voices of teachers and teaching assistants. *Support for Learning*, 26(2): 56–63.

Goodall, C. (2010) *The experiences, attitudes and knowledge of post-primary school teachers in one education and library board to teaching children with Autistic Spectrum Disorder/Asperger Syndrome*. Dissertation collection, Queen's University, Belfast.

Goodall, C. (2012) A question of inclusion. *Special Educational Needs*, 57: 82–83.

Goodall, C. (2015a) How do we create ASD-friendly schools? A dilemma of placement. *Support for Learning*, 30(4): 305–326.

Goodall, C. (2015b) Excluded by inclusion. *Special Educational Needs Magazine*, 74: 70–72.

Goodall, C. (2015c) Is it time for ASD specific schools? *UTU News*, Spring: 16–17.

Goodall, C. (2018a) Inclusion is a feeling, not a place: A qualitative study exploring autistic young people's conceptualisations of inclusion. *International Journal of Inclusive Education*. Online first doi:10.1080/13603116.2018.1523475.

Goodall, C. (2018b) Mainstream is not for all: The educational experiences of autistic young people. *Disability and Society*, 33(10): 1661–1665

Goodall, C. (2018c) "I felt closed in and like I couldn't breathe": A qualitative study exploring the mainstream educational experiences of autistic young people. *Autism and Developmental Language Impairments*, 3: 1–16.

Goodall, C. (2018d) Mainstream is not for all: The educational experiences of autistic young people. *Disability and Society*, 33(10): 1661–1665

Goodall, C. (2019) 'There is more flexibility to meet my needs': Educational experiences of autistic young people in mainstream and alternative education provision. *Support for Learning*, 34: 4–33.

Goodall, C. and MacKenzie, A. (2018) What about my voice? Autistic young girls' experiences of mainstream school. *European Journal of Special Needs Education*. 33(10): 1661–1665.

Grandin, T. (1996) Interview with Dr Stephen Edelson. www.autism.com/advocacy_grandin_interview (last accessed on 14th July 2017).

Grandin, T. (2006) *Thinking in pictures, expanded edition: My life with autism.* New York: Vintage Books.

Grandin, T. (2009) "How does visual thinking work in the mind of a person with autism? A personal account." *Philosophical Transactions of the Royal Society of London B: Biological Sciences*, 364(1522): 1437–1442.

Guba, E.G. (1981) Criteria for assessing the trustworthiness of naturalistic inquiries. *Educational Communication and Technology*, 29(2): 75–91.

Gunn, K. and Delafield-Butt, J. (2016) Teaching children with autism spectrum disorder with restricted interests: A review of evidence for best practice. *Review of Educational Research*, 86(2): 408–430.

Haas, K., Costley, D., Falkmer, M., Richdale, A., Sofronoff, K. and Falkmer, T. (2016) Factors influencing the research participation of adults with autism spectrum disorders. *Journal of Autism and Developmental Disorders*, 46(5): 1793–1805.

Hammersley, M. (2017) Childhood studies: A sustainable paradigm? *Childhood*, 24(1): 113–127.

Hanson, K. (2017) Embracing the past: 'Been', 'being' and 'becoming' children. *Childhood*, 24(3): 281–285.

Harrington, C., Foster, M., Rodger, S. and Ashburner, J. (2013) Engaging young people with Autism Spectrum Disorder in research interviews. *British Journal of Learning Disability*, 48: 1–9.

Hart, R. (1992) *Children's participation: From tokenism to citizenship*. Florence: UNICEF.

Hart, R. (2008) Stepping back from 'The ladder': reflections on a model of participatory work with children. In Reid, A., Jensen, B.B., Nikel, J. and Simovska, V. (Eds.) *Participation and learning: Perspectives on education and the environment, health and sustainability* (pp. 19–31). New York: Springer.

Hart, S. and Drummond, M.J. (2014) Learning without limits: Constructing a pedagogy free from determinist beliefs about ability (pp. 439–458). In Florian, L. (Ed.) *The SAGE handbook of special education* (2nd edition), Volume 2. London: Sage.

Hart, S., Dixon, A., Drummond, M.J. and McIntyre, D. (2004) *Learning without limits*. Maidenhead, UK: Open University Press.

Hayes, J.A., Baylot Casey, L., Williamson, R., Black, T. and Winsor, D. (2013) Educators' readiness to teach children with autism spectrum disorder in an inclusive classroom. *The Researcher*, 25(1): 67–78

Hebron, J. and Humphrey, N. (2014) Mental health difficulties among young people on the autistic spectrum in mainstream secondary schools: A comparative study. *Journal of Research in Special Educational Needs*, 14(1): 22–32.

Hill, M. (2006) Children's voices on ways of having a voice: Children's and young people's perspectives on methods used in research and consultation. *Childhood*, 13(1): 69–89.

Hirvikoski, T., Mittendorfer-Rutz, E., Boman, M., Larsson, H., Lichtenstein, P. and Bölte, S. (2016) Premature mortality in autism spectrum disorder. *The British Journal of Psychiatry*, 208(3): 232–238.

Hodge, N., Rice, E.J. and Reidy, L. (2019) "They're told all the time they're different": How educators understand development of sense of self for autistic pupils. *Disability and Society*, https://doi.org/10.1080/09687599.2019.1594700

Hollenweger, J. (2014) Reconciling "all" within "special" away forward towards a more inclusive thinking. In Kiuppis, F. and Hausstatter, R.J. (Eds.) *Inclusive education twenty years after Salamanca*. New York: Peter Lang Publishing.

Honeybourne, V. (2015) Listening to pupils. *Special Educational Needs*, 74: 58–59.

Hornby, G. (2012) Inclusive education for children with Special Educational Needs in New Zealand: A critique of policy and practice in New Zealand. *Journal of International and Comparative Education*, 1(1): 52–60.

Hornby, G. (2015) Inclusive special education: Development of a new theory for the education of children with special educational needs and disabilities. *British Journal of Special Education*, 42(3): 234–256.

House of Commons Education and Skills Committee (2006) Special Educational Needs: Third report of session 2005–06. London: The Stationary Office.

Humphrey, N. and Hebron, J. (2015) Bullying of children and adolescents with autism spectrum conditions: A 'state of the field' review. *International Journal of Inclusive Education*, 19(8): 845–862.

Humphrey, N. and Lewis, S. (2008a) What does 'inclusion' mean for pupils on the autistic spectrum in mainstream secondary schools? *Journal of Research in Special Educational Needs*, 8(3): 132–140.

Humphrey, N. and Lewis, S. (2008b) 'Make me normal': The views and experiences of pupils on the autistic spectrum in mainstream secondary schools. *Autism*, 12: 23–46.

Humphrey, N. and Parkinson, G. (2006) Research on interventions for children and young people on the autistic spectrum: a critical perspective. *Journal of Research in Special Educational Needs*, 6(2): 76–86.

Humphrey, N. and Symes, W. (2010) Perceptions of social support and experience of bullying among pupils with autistic spectrum disorders in mainstream secondary schools. *European Journal of Special Needs Education*, 25(1): 77–91.

Humphrey, N. and Symes, W. (2011) Peer interaction patterns among adolescents with autistic spectrum disorders (ASDs) in mainstream schools. *Autism: An International Journal of Research and Practice*, 15(3): 1–23.

Humphrey, N. and Symes, W. (2012) Bullying and autism: Helping kids cope with getting excluded. http://www.education.com/reference/article/bullying-a utism/ (last accessed on 7th April 2016).

Humphrey, N. and Symes, W. (2013) Inclusive education for pupils with autistic spectrum disorders in secondary mainstream schools: Teacher attitudes, experience and knowledge. *International Journal of Inclusive Education*, 17 (1): 32–46.

Hurlbutt-Eastman, K. (2017) Teaching the child with exceptional needs at home (pp. 222–245). In Gaither, M. (Ed.) *The Wiley handbook of home education*. London: John Wiley and Sons.

Imray, P. and Colley, A. (2017) *Inclusion is dead: long live inclusion*. London: Routledge.

James, A. (2012) Seeking the analytic imagination: reflections on the process of interpreting qualitative data. *Qualitative Research*, 13(5): 562–577.

Jang, J., Matson, J.L., Adams, H.L., Konst, M.J., Cervantes, P.E. and Goldin, R.L. (2014) What are the ages of persons studied in autism research: A 20-year review. *Research in Autism Spectrum Disorders*, 8: 1756–1760.

Jordan, R. (1999) *Autistic spectrum disorders: An introductory handbook for practitioners*. London: David Fulton Publishers.

Jordan, R. (2005) Autistic spectrum disorders (pp. 110–122). In Lewis, A. and Norwich, B. (Eds.) *Special teaching for special children? Pedagogies for inclusion*. Maidenhead, UK: Open University Press.

Jordan, R. (2008) Autistic spectrum disorders: a challenge and a model for inclusion in education. *British Journal of Special Education*, 35(1): 11–15.

Kanner, L. (1943) Autistic disturbances of affective contact. *Nervous Child*, 2: 217–250.

Kapp, S.K., Gillepsie-Lynch, K., Sherman, L.E. and Hutman, T. (2013) Deficit, difference, or both? Autism and neurodiversity. *Developmental Psychology*, 49 (1): 59–71.

Kasari, C., Freeman, F.N., Bauminger, N. and Alkin, M.C. (1999) Parental perspectives on inclusion: effects of autism and Down syndrome. *Journal of Autism and Developmental Disorders*, 29(4): 297–305.

Keane, E., Aldridge, F.J., Costley, D. and Clark, T. (2012) Students with autism in regular classes: a long-term follow-up study of a satellite class transition model. *Journal of Inclusive Education*, 16(10): 1001–1017.

Kenny, L., Hattersley, C., Molins, B., Buckley, C., Povey, C. and Pellicano, E. (2016) Which terms should be used to describe autism? Perspectives from the UK autism community. *Autism*, 20(4): 442–462.

Kidd, T. and Kaczmarek, F. (2010) The experiences of mothers' home educating their children with autism spectrum disorder. *Issues in Educational Research*, 20(3): 257–275.

Kim, Y.S., Leventhal, B.L., Koh, Y.J., Fombonne, E., Laska, E., Lim, E.C. and Grinker, R.R. (2011) Prevalence of autism spectrum disorders in a total population sample. *American Journal of Psychiatry*, 168: 904–912.

Komulainen, S. (2007) The ambiguity of the child's voice in social research. *Childhood*, 14(1): 11–28.

Kreiser, N.L. and White, S.W. (2014) ASD in females: Are we overstating the gender difference in diagnosis? *Clinical Child Family Psychology*, 17: 67–84.

Kucharczyk, S.Reutebuch, C.K., Carter, E.W., Hedges, S., Zein, F.E., Fan, H. and Gustafson, J.R. (2015) Addressing the needs of adolescents with autism spectrum disorder: considerations and complexities for High School interventions. *Exceptional Children*, 81(3): 329–349.

Kvale, S. (1996). *Interviews: An introduction to qualitative research interviewing.* Thousand Oaks, CA: Sage.

Lai, M.C., Lambardo, M.V., Auyeung, B., Chakrabarti, B. and Baron-Cohen, S. (2015) Sex/gender differences and autism. *Journal of the American Academy of Child and Adolescent Psychiatry*, 54(1): 11–24

Lai, M.C., Lombardo, M.V., Ruigrok, A.N., Chakrabarti, B., Auyeung, B., Szatmari, P., Happé, F. and Baron-Cohen, S. (2017) Quantifying and exploring camouflaging in men and women with autism. *Autism*, 21(6): 690–702.

Lansdown, G. (2011) *Every child's right to be heard: a resource guide on the UN Convention on the Right of the Child, General Comment No. 12.* London: Save the Children.

Lauchlan, F. and Greig, S. (2015) Educational inclusion in England: Origins, perspectives and current directions. *Support for Learning*, 30(1): 69–82.

Le Blanc, R. and Volkers, H. (2008) *What you should know about autism spectrum disorders: Signs, symptoms, treatments and effects on daily life.* Bradenton, FL: Booklocker.

Lee, F.L.M., Young, A.S., Tracey, D. and Barker, K. (2015) Inclusion of children with special needs in early childhood education: What teacher characteristics matter. *Topics in Early Childhood Special Education*, 35(2): 79–88.

Leitch, R. (2008) Creatively researching children's narratives through images and drawing (pp. 37–58). In Thomson, P. (Ed.) *Doing visual research with children and young people.* London: Routledge.

Levi, S. (2005) Ableism (pp. 1–3). In Albrecht, G.L. (Ed.) *Encyclopedia of disability*, Volume 1. Thousand Oaks, CA: Sage Publications.

Levy, A. and Perry, A. (2011) Outcomes in Adolescents and Adults with Autism: A review of the Literature. *Research in Autism Spectrum Disorders*, 5(4): 1271–1282.

Lewis, A. (2009) Methodological issues in exploring the ideas of children with autism concerning self and spirituality. *Journal of Religion and Disability Health*, 13: 64–76.

Lewis, A. (2010) Silence in the context of child voices. *Children and Society*, 24 (1): 14–23.

Lincoln, Y.S. and Guba, E.G. (1985) *Naturalistic inquiry.* Beverly Hills, CA: Sage.

Lindsay, S., Proulx, M., Thomson, N. and Scott, H. (2013) Educators' challenges of including children with autism spectrum disorder in mainstream classrooms. *International Journal of Disability, Development and Education*, 60(4): 347–362.

Linton, A-C., Germundsson, P., Heimann, M. and Danermark, B. (2015) The role of experience in teachers' social representation of students with autism spectrum disorder (Asperger). *Cogent Education*, 2: 1–18.

Livingston, L.A., Colvert, E., Bolton, P. and Happé, F. (2019) Good social skills despite poor theory of mind: Exploring compensation in autism spectrum disorder. *Journal of Child Psychology and Psychiatry*, 60(1): 102–110.

Locke, J., Ishijima, E.H., Kasari, C. and London, N. (2010) Loneliness, friendship quality and the social networks of adolescents with high-functioning autism in an inclusive school setting. *Journal of Research in Special Educational Needs*, 10(2): 74–81.

Low, C. (2007) A defense of moderate inclusion (pp. 3–14). In Cigman, R. (Ed.) *Included or excluded? The challenge of mainstream for some SEN children.* London: Routledge.

Lundy, L. (2006) Mainstreaming children's rights in to and through education in a society emerging from conflict. *International Journal of Children's Rights*, 14: 339–362.

Lundy, L. (2007) Voice is not enough: Conceptualising Article 12 of the United Nations Convention on the Rights of the Child. *British Educational Research Journal*, 33(6): 927–942.

Lundy, L. (2018) In defence of Tokenism? Children's rights to participate in collective decision making. *Childhood*, 25(3): 340–354.

Lundy, L. (2012) Children's rights and educational policy in Europe: implementation of the UNCRC. *Oxford Review of Education*, 38(4): 393–411.

Lundy, L. and Kilkelly, U. (2006) Children's rights in action: using the UN Convention on the Rights of the Child as an auditing tool. *Child and Family Law Quarterly*, 18(3): 331–350.

Lundy, L. and McEvoy, L. (2011) Children's rights and research processes: Assisting children to (in)formed views. *Childhood*, 19(1): 129–141.

Lundy, L. and McEvoy, L. (2012) Childhood, the United Nations Convention on the Rights of the Child and research: what constitutes a rights-based approach (pp. 75–91). In Freeman, M. (Ed.) *Law and childhood.* Oxford, UK: Oxford University Press.

Lundy, L. and Stalford, H. (2013) *Children's rights and participation: Background paper for Eurochild Annual Conference 2013*. Eurochild.

Lynch, S.L. and Irvine, A.N. (2009) Inclusive education and best practice for children with autism spectrum disorder: Sn integrated approach. *International Journal of Inclusive Education*, 13(8): 845–859.

Majoko, T. (2016) Inclusion of children with autism spectrum disorders: Listening and hearing to voices from the grassroots. *Journal of Autism and Developmental Disorders*, 46(4): 1429–1440.

McGillicuddy, S. and O'Donnell, G.M. (2014) Teaching students with autism spectrum disorder in mainstream post-primary schools in the Republic of Ireland. *International Journal of Inclusive Education*. 18(4): 323–344.

McGregor, E. and Campbell, E. (2001) The attitudes of teachers in Scotland to the integration of children with autism into mainstream schools. *Autism*, 5: 189–207.

McMillan, J.H. and Schumacher, S. (2006) *Research in education: Evidence-based inquiry*. New York: Pearson Education.

McNaught, C. and Lam, P. (2010) Using Wordle as a supplementary research tool. *The Qualitative Report*, 15(3): 630–643.

Mannion, G. (2007) Going spatial, going relational: why listening to children and children's participation needs reframing. *Discourse: Studies in the Cultural Politics of Education*, 28(3): 405–420.

Martin, D. (2012) The ever-changing social perception of autism spectrum disorders in the United States. *Journal of Exploration in Social Sciences*, 1: 1–22.

Martin, T., Dixon, R., Verenikina, I. and Costley, D. (2019) Transitioning primary school students with Autism Spectrum Disorder from a special education setting to a mainstream classroom: successes and difficulties. *International Journal of Inclusive Education*, 1–16. https://www.tandfonline.com/doi/full/10.1080/13603116.2019.1568597

Mauthner, M. (1997) Methodological aspects of collecting data from children: Lessons from three research projects. *Children and Society*, 11(1): 16–28.

Mazefsky, C.A., Herrington, J., Siegel, M., Scarpa, A., Maddos, B.B., Scahill, L. and White, S.W. (2013) The role of emotion regulation in autism spectrum disorder. *Journal of American Academy of Child and Adolescent Psychiatry*, 52 (7): 679–688

Meyers, A.B. and Sylvester, B.A. (2006) The role of qualitative research methods in evidence-based practice. *Communiqué*, 34(5): 26–28.

Michailakis, D. and Reich, W. (2009) Dilemmas of inclusive education. *European Journal of Disability Research*, 3: 23–44.

Milton, D.E.M. (2012) On the ontological status of autism: The 'double empathy problem'. *Disability and Society*, 27(6): 883–887.

Milton, D.E.M. (2014) Autistic expertise: A critical reflection on the production of knowledge in autism studies. *Autism*, 18(7): 794–802. doi:10.1177/1362361314525281.

Milton, D.E.M. (2017) Zen and the art of aut-ethnography: A tribute to Robert M. Pirsig. *Disability and Society*, 32(10): 1671–1676.

Milton, D., Mills, R. and Pellicano, E. (2014) Ethics and autism: Where is the autistic voice? Commentary on Post et al. *Journal of Autism and Developmental Disorders*, 44(10): 2650–2651.

Modabbernia, A., Velthorst, E. and Reichenberg, A. (2017) Environmental risk factors for autism: An evidence-based review of systematic reviews and meta-analyses. *Molecular Autism*, 8(1): 13.

Monteith, M., McLaughlin, E., Milner, S. and Hamilton, L. (2002). *Is anyone listening? Childhood disability and public services in Northern Ireland*. Belfast: Barnardos.

Morewood, G.D. (2012) Is the 'inclusive SENCo' still a possibility? A personal perspective. *Support for Learning*, 27(2): 73–76.

Morewood, G.D., Humphrey, N. and Symes, W. (2011) Mainstreaming autism: Making it work. *Good Autism Practice Journal*, 12(2): 62–68.

Moyse, R. and Porter, J. (2015) The experience of the hidden curriculum for autistic girls at mainstream primary schools. *European Journal of Special Needs Education*, 30(2): 187–201.

Muhle, R.A., Reed, H.E., Stratigos, K.A. and Veenstra-VanderWeele, J. (2018) The emerging clinical neuroscience of autism spectrum disorder: A review. *JAMA Psychiatry*, 75(5): 514–523.

Murray, D. and Lawson, W. (2007) Inclusion through technology for autistic children. In Cigman, R. (Ed.) *Included or excluded? The challenge of mainstream for some SEN children*. London: Routledge.

National Autistic Society (2006) *Autism spectrum disorder: A resource pack for school staff*. NAS.

National Autistic Society Northern Ireland (2012) *A* for autism: Make every school a good school*. National Autistic Society.

Northern Ireland Commissioner for Children and Young People (2007) Try living in our world. Young people with Asperger syndrome: A review of needs and services. NICCY.

O'Hagan, S. and Hebron, J. (2017) Perceptions of friendship among adolescents with autism spectrum conditions in a mainstream high school resource provision. *European Journal of Special Needs Education*, 32(3): 314–328.

Oliver, M. (1990) *The politics of disablement*. Basingstoke, UK: MacMillan.

Oliver, M. (1996) *Understanding disability: From theory to practice*. Basingstoke, UK: Palgrave.

O'Neil, S. (2008) The meaning of autism: Beyond disorder. *Disability and Society*, 23(7): 787–799.

Pandolfi, V., Magyar, C.L. and Dill, C.A. (2012) An initial psychometric evaluation of the CBCL 6–18 sample of youth with autism spectrum disorders. *Research in Autism Spectrum Disorders*, 6(1): 96–108.

Park, M., Chitiyo, M. and Choi, Y.S. (2010) Examining pre-service teachers' attitudes towards children with autism in the USA. *Journal of Research in Special Educational Needs*, 10(2): 107–114.

Parsons, S. (2015) Why are we an ignored group? Mainstream educational experiences and current life satisfaction of adults on the autism spectrum from an online survey. *International Journal of Inclusive Education*, 19(4): 397–421.

Parsons, S., Sherwood, G. and Abbott, C. (2016) Informed consent with children and young people in social research: Is there scope for innovation? *Children and Society*, 30(2): 132–145.

Parsons, S., Guldberg, K., MacLeod, A., JonesG., Prunty, A. and Balfe, T. (2011) International review of the evidence of best practice in educational provision for children on the autism spectrum. *European Journal of Special Needs Education*, 26(1): 47–63.

Pellicano, E. and Stears, M. (2011) Bridging autism, science and society: Moving toward an ethically informed approach to autism research. *Autism Research*, 4: 271–278.

Pellicano, L., Bölte, S. and Stahmer, A. (2018) The current illusion of educational inclusion. *Autism*, 22(4): 386–387.

Pellicano, E., Crane, L., Gaudion, K. and the Shaping Autism Research team. (2017) *Participatory autism research: A starter pack*. London: UCL Institute of Education.

Poon, K.K., Soon, S., Wong, M-E., Kaur, S., Khaw, J., Ng, Z. and Tan, C.S. (2014) What is school like? Perspective of Singaporean youth with high-functioning autism spectrum disorders. *International Journal of Inclusive Education*, 18(10): 1069–1081.

Preece, D. and Jordan, R. (2010) Obtaining the views of children and young people with autism spectrum disorders about their experience of daily life and social care support. *British Journal of Learning Disabilities*, 38(1): 10–20.

Ravet, J. (2011) Inclusive/exclusive? Contradictory perspectives on autism and inclusion: the case for an integrative position. *International Journal of Inclusive Education*, 15(6): 667–682.

Reiter, S. and Vitani, T. (2007) Inclusion of pupils with autism: The effect of an intervention program on the regular pupils' burnout, attitudes and quality of mediation. *Autism*, 11(4): 321–333.

Rioux, M. (2014) Disability rights in education (pp. 131–147). In Florian, L. (Ed.) *The SAGE handbook of special education* (2nd edition), Volume 1. London: Sage.

Robinson, C. and Taylor, C. (2013) Student voice as a contested practice: Power and participation in two student voice projects. *Improving Schools*, 16 (1): 32–46.

Rogers, C. (2007) Experiencing an 'inclusive' education: parents and their children with 'special educational needs'. *British Journal of Sociology of Education*, 28(1): 55–68.

Rose, A.J. and Rudolph, K.D. (2006) A review of sex differences in peer relationship processes: Potential trade-offs for the emotional and behavioural development of girls and boys. *Psychological Bulletin*, 132: 98–131.

Rose, D.H., Gravel, J.W. and Gordan, D.T. (2014) Universal design for learning (pp. 475–491). In Florian, L. (Ed.) *The SAGE handbook of special education* (2nd edition), Volume 2. London: Sage.

Rose, R. and Shevlin, M. (2017) A sense of belonging: Children's views of acceptance in 'inclusive' mainstream schools. *International Journal of Whole Schooling*, Special Issue: 65–80.

Ruble, L., Dalrymple, N. and McGrew, J. (2010) The effects of consultation on Individualised Education Program outcomes for young children with autism: The collaborative model for promoting competence and success. *Journal of Early Intervention*, 32: 286–301.

Safran, J.S. (2002) Supporting students with Asperger's syndrome in general education. *Teaching Exceptional Children*, 34(5): 60–66.

Saggers, B., Hwang, Y-S. and Mercer, L. (2011) Your voice counts: Listening to the voice of high school students with autism spectrum disorders. *Australasian Journal of Special Education*, 35(2): 173–190.

Sciutto, M., Richwine, S., Mentrikoski, J. and Niedzwiecki, K. (2012) A qualitative analysis of school experience of students with autism spectrum disorders. *Focus on Autism and Other Developmental Disabilities*, 27: 177–188.

Scott-Barrett, J., Cebula, K. and Florian, L. (2018) Listening to young people with autism: Learning from researcher experiences. *International Journal of Research and Method in Education*, 1–22. doi:10.1080/1743727X.2018.1462791.

Scottish Executive (2006) *Draft children's services (Scotland) bill consultation*. Edinburgh: Scottish Executive.

Scottish Government (2013) Getting It Right For Every Child (GIRFEC). https://www.gov.scot/policies/girfec/ (last accessed 15th May 2019).

Segall, M.J. and Campbell, J.M. (2012) Factors relating to education professionals' classroom practices for the inclusion of students with autism spectrum disorders. *Research in Autism Spectrum Disorders*, 6(3): 1156–1167.

Shier, H. (2001) Pathways to participation: Openings, opportunities and obligations. A new model for enhancing children's participation in decision-making, in line with Article 12.1 of the United Nations Convention on the Rights of the Child. *Children and Society*, 15: 107–117.

Shier, H. (2006) Pathways to participation revisited: Nicaragua perspective. New Zealand Association for Intermediate and Middle Schooling. http://www.harryshier.net/docs/Shier-Pathways_to_Participation_Revisited_NZ2006.pdf (last accessed 2nd April 2019).

Slee, R. (2011) *The irregular school: Exclusion, schooling and inclusive education*. Abingdon, UK: Routledge.

Smith, A.B. (2012) Links to theory and advocacy: children's rights and early childhood education. *Australasian Journal of Early Childhood*, 32(3): 1–8.

Solomon, M., Miller, M., Taylor, S.L., Hinshaw, S.P. and Carter, C.S. (2012) Autism symptoms and internalizing psychopathology in girls and boys with autism spectrum disorders. *Journal of Autism and Developmental Disorders*, 42(1): 48–59.

Special Educational Needs and Disability Act (Northern Ireland) (2016) http://www.legislation.gov.uk/nia/2016/8/contents (last accessed 15th May 2019).

SpillersJ.L.H., SensuiL.M. and LintonK.F. (2014) Concerns about identity and services among people with autism and Asperger's regarding DSM-5 Changes. *Journal of Social Work in Disability and Rehabilitation*, 13: 37–41.

Spratt, J. and Florian, L. (2015) Inclusive pedagogy: From learning to action. Supporting each individual in the context of 'everybody'. *Teaching and Teacher Education*, 49: 89–96.

Spratt, J., Florian, L. and Rouse, M. (2010) Enacting inclusion: finding spaces for beginning teachers to apply the principles of inclusive pedagogy. Paper presented to the European Conference for Educational Research, University of Helsinki, August 2010.

Sproston, K., Sedgewick, F. and Crane, L. (2017) Autistic girls and school inclusion: perspectives of students and their parents. *Autism and Developmental Language Impairments*, 2: 1–14.

Sreckovic, M.A., Brunsting, N.C. and Able, H. (2014) Victimization of students with autism spectrum disorder: A review of prevalence and risk factors. *Research in Autism Spectrum Disorders*, 8: 1155–1167.

Stratheam, L. (2009) The elusive aetiology of autism: Nature and nurture? *Frontiers in Behavioral Neuroscience*, 3(11): 1–3.

Swain, J. and French, S. (2000) Towards an affirmative model of disability. *Disability and Society*, 15: 569–582.

Taylor, F. (2005) *A fair hearing? Researching young people's involvement in the school exclusion process*. London: Save the Children.

Terry, P.M. (1996) Preparing educational leaders to eradicate the "isms". Paper presented at the Annual International Congress on Challenges to Education: Balancing Unity and Diversity in a Changing World, Palm Beach, Aruba, July 10–12. https://files.eric.ed.gov/fulltext/ED400612.pdf

Thomas, D.R. (2003) A general inductive approach to qualitative data analysis. University of Auckland, Australia. http://www.frankumstein.com/PDF/Psychology/Inductive%20Content%20Analysis.pdf (last accessed 5th February 2019).

Thomas, G. (2013) A review of thinking and research about inclusive education policy, with suggestions for a new kind of inclusive thinking. *British Educational Research Journal*, 39(3): 473–490.

Thomas, G. and Loxley, A. (2007) *Deconstructing special education and constructing inclusion* (2nd edition). Maidenhead, UK: Open University Press.

Timpson, E. (2019) *Timpson review of school exclusion* (CP92). London: Department for Education.

Tobin, H., Staunton, S., Mandy, W., Skuse, D., Hellriegel, J., Baykaner, O. Anderson, S. and Murin, M. (2012) A qualitative examination of parental experiences of the transition to mainstream secondary school for children with an autism spectrum disorder. *Educational and Child Psychology*, 29(1): 75–85.

Tomaševski, K. (2001a) *Annual report of the special rapporteur on the right of education. E/CN.4/2001/52.* Geneva: United Nations.

Tomaševski, K. (2001b) *Human rights obligations: Making education available, accessible, acceptable and adaptable* (Rights to Education Primers, no.3). Gothenburg, Sweden: Novum Grafiska. http://www.right-to-education.org/sites/right-to-education.org/files/resource-attachments/Tomasevski_Primer%203.pdf (last accessed 16th June 2016).

Treweek, C., Wood, C., Martin, J. and Freeth, M. (2018) Autistic people's perspectives on stereotypes: An interpretative phenomenological analysis. *Autism*, 23(3): 759–769

UNESCO (1994) Inclusive education: The Salamanca statement and framework for action on special needs education. Paris: UNESCO.

UNESCO (2009) Policy guidelines on inclusion in education. Paris: UNESCO.

United Nations (1989) Convention on the Rights of the Child. Geneva: Office of the High Commissioner, United Nations.

United Nations (1997) Convention on the Rights of the Child general discussions on the rights of children with disabilities. UN/CRC/C/66, Annex V. Geneva: United Nations.

United Nations (2003) Statement of common understanding on a human rights-based approach to development co-operation. Geneva: United Nations. http://www.unicef.org/sowc04/files/AnnexB.pdf (last accessed 28th July 2016).

United Nations (2006a) Convention on the Rights of Persons with Disabilities and optional protocol. Geneva: Office of the High Commissioner, United Nations.

United Nations (2006b) United Nations Committee on the Rights of the Child general comment No. 9 on the rights of children with disabilities. CRC/C/GC/9. Geneva: United Nations.

United Nations (2007) Report of the Special Rapporteur on the Right to Education: The Right to Education of Persons with Disabilities. UN Doc A/HRC/4/29 (19 February 2007). Geneva: United Nations.

United Nations (2009) United Nations Committee on the Rights of the Child General Comment No. 12, the Right of the Child to be Heard. CRC/C/GC/12. Geneva: United Nations.

United Nations (2016) United Nations Committee on the Rights of Persons with Disabilities General Comment No. 4, on Article 24: Right to inclusive education. CRPD/C/GC/4. Geneva: United Nations.

United Nations (2017) Report of the Special Rapporteur on the right to education. A/72/496. Geneva: United Nations.

UTV News (2016) http://www.u.tv/News/2016/02/14/Hamilton-announces-extra-2m-for-autism-services-54046 (last accessed 18th March 2016).

Wainscot, J.J., Naylor, P., Sutcliffe, D.T. and Williams, J.V. (2008) Relationship with peers and use of the school environment of mainstream secondary school pupils with Asperger syndrome (high-functioning autism): A case–control study. *International Journal of Psychology and Psychological Therapy*, 8(1): 25–28

Warnock, M. (2005) *Special educational needs: A new look*. London: Philosophy of Education Society of Great Britain.

Westcott, H.L. and Littleton, K.S. (2005) Exploring meaning in interview with children (pp. 141–157). In Greene, S. and Hogan, D. (Eds.) *Researching children's experiences: Methods and approaches*. London: Sage.

White, S.W., Oswald, D., Ollendick, T. and Scahill, L. (2009) Anxiety in children and adolescents with autism spectrum disorders. *Clinical Psychology Review*, 29(3): 216–229.

Wing, L. (1981) Asperger's syndrome: A clinical account. *Psychological Medicine*, 11: 115–129.

Wing, L. (1996) *The autistic spectrum: A guide for parents and professionals.* London: Constable and Co.

Wing, L. (1997) *The autistic spectrum.* Oxford, UK: Pergamon.

Wing, L. (2007) Children with autistic spectrum disorders (pp. 23–33). In Cigman, R. (Ed.) *Included or excluded? The challenge of mainstream for some SEN children.* London: Routledge.

Wing, L. and Gould, J. (1979) Severe impairments of social interaction and associated abnormalities in children: Epidemiology and classification. *Journal of Autism and Developmental Disorders*, 9: 11–29.

Winstone, N., Huntington, C., Goldsack, L., Kyrou, E. and Millward, L. (2014) Eliciting rich dialogue through the use of activity-orientated interviews: Exploring self-identity in autistic young people. *Childhood*, 21(2): 190–206.

Winter-Messiers, M., Herr, C., Wood, C., Brooks, A., Gates, M., Houston, T. and Tingstad, K. (2007) How far can Brian ride the daylight 4449 Express? A strength-based model of Asperger syndrome based on special interest areas. *Focus on Autism and Other Developmental Disabilities*, 22(2): 67–79.

Wood, R. (2019) Autism, intense interests and support in school: From wasted efforts to shared understandings. *Educational Review*, doi:10.1080/00131911.2019.1566213.

Woods, R. (2017) Exploring how the social model of disability can be re-invigorated for autism: In response to Jonathan Levitt. *Disability and Society*, 32(7): 1090–1095.

Zermatten, J. (2010) The best interests of the child principle: Literal analysis and function. *International Journal of Children's Rights*, 18: 483–499.

Index

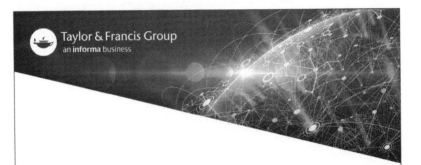

Printed in Great Britain
by Amazon

79819463R00097